Laws and policies to contrast and prevent Gender-Based Violence Against Women

A comparative analysis between Spain and Italy (1993-2015)

Stellamarina Donato
LUMSA University of Rome, Italy

Women's Studies

VERNON PRESS

In the Americas:
Vernon Press
1000 N West Street, Suite 1200,
Wilmington, Delaware 19801
United States

In the rest of the world:
Vernon Press
C/Sancti Espiritu 17,
Malaga, 29006
Spain

Women's Studies

Library of Congress Control Number: 2023942825

ISBN: 978-1-64889-932-4

Also available: 978-1-64889-761-0 [Hardback]; 978-1-64889-783-2 [PDF, E-Book]

Product and company names mentioned in this work are the trademarks of their respective owners. While every care has been taken in preparing this work, neither the authors nor Vernon Art and Science Inc. may be held responsible for any loss or damage caused or alleged to be caused directly or indirectly by the information contained in it.

Every effort has been made to trace all copyright holders, but if any have been inadvertently overlooked the publisher will be pleased to include any necessary credits in any subsequent reprint or edition.

Cover design by Vernon Press using elements designed by Freepik.

The figures that appear in this book are available for download at https://vernonpress.com/book/1841

Table of contents

Table of acronyms

CoE	Council of Europe
Council of the EU	Council of the European Union
DEVAW	Declaration on the Elimination of Violence Against Women
EC	European Commission
EP	European Parliament
ESC	Economic and Social Council (UN)
EU	European Union
GA	General Assembly
GBVAW	Gender-Based Violence Against Women
GR	Government Responsiveness
GV	Gender Violence
HRC	Human Rights Council
MDGs	Millennium Development Goals
MEP(s)	Member(s) of the European Parliament
MS(s)	Member State(s)
MVAW	Male Violence Against Women
SDGs	Sustainable Development Goals
UN	United Nations
UNE	United Nations Entity for Gender Equality
VAW	Violence Against Women
VTW	Violence Towards Women

List of figures and tables

Figures

Tables

List of Figures and tables

Foreword

Violence against women is not a new phenomenon in human history but it has gained scientific recognition in the last three decades (for example, the journal *Violence against Women* was established in 1995). The interest of sociological research has increased along with the growing intolerance of the general public toward any form of violence; but above all, it has grown due to the affirmation of women's rights. Violence against women is now a central issue on the agenda of global women's movements, and is part of a powerful discourse that, over the past three decades, has shifted from the cognitive framework of women's dignity to that of human rights. With its burden of injustice and pain, the concept of violence intersects inquiry into further social issues: family structure, child abuse, increased policy effectiveness, women's empowerment, gendered roles, and many others. This crossroads of questions about society, policy-making, and inequality challenge sociological research.

Today, violence against women is a central issue on the agenda of women's movements. Beginning with the 1993 Vienna Declaration on Human Rights and, two years later, the 1995 Beijing Conference, a new definition has emerged as part of a comprehensive narrative that holds together diverse actions (such as, for example, stalking, psychological manipulation, and femicide) that summarizes in a single category certain underlying themes: the critique of male domination, the demand for equality, the protection of victims, and the mobilization for a more just and equitable society. This set of categories is a strong program which also works as an interpretive paradigm of contemporary societies. The collective actors of the program are international and regional organizations, women's and feminist movements, and national governments, which can plan, fund, or hinder policy actions aimed at raising awareness, preventing violence, and protecting the victims.

Stellamarina Donato's book fits into this context. In particular, using a multi-method and comparative approach, the book focuses on the development of policy-making in Spain and Italy from 1993 to 2015. In the academic literature on welfare policies, these two countries are often placed in the single category of "Southern European countries." Instead, the book shows clearly why and how they differ significantly in terms of women's movement action and government responsiveness on violence.

An original feature of this book is the analysis of the "soft power" of international and regional policies on national territories. As the author writes, "language is a powerful tool [...] but it is also a place of struggle." A central part of the book is devoted to the investigation of the language of policy-making, the different theoretical frames and the practical consequences of using concept-driven terms such as gender-based violence, violence against women or male violence against women as a reference for policies. The author collects and analyzes the most relevant policy documents of the United Nations Organization, the Council of Europe, and the European Union on violence against women, showing that they greatly influence the responsiveness of national governments.

Today, violence against women is a category for reading and evaluating contemporary societies, which was unprecedented and concerned behaviors previously placed in the sphere of private actions. Policies to prevent and combat violence are the result of processes of change, involving power relations, gender behaviors and sexuality. These are slow processes by their nature because they involve a profound culture shift. Sociology and policy studies highlight how, since the 1970s, the actors in the culture shift have been feminist and women's movements that have identified violence as one of the most important issues of aggregation and identity and have become the main stakeholders urging action on policy making. But despite the growing international consensus around the nature of violence against women and its social cost, important differences remain in the policies put in place at the national level, and the speed of change is extremely different from country to country. Consequently, cross-national comparisons are useful because they illuminate actions that are taking place in one context but do not occur in the other, and they provide us with a better understanding of obstacles and facilitators toward the cultural shift which is embedded in policy change. This book is an extremely valuable tool in clarifying the broader context and multiple actors at play in violence prevention at the international, regional and national levels and it displays a methodology and theoretical elaboration which can be used for other comparative case-studies.

Consuelo Corradi,
LUMSA University, Italy

Introduction

The will to understand the lacks and flaws in the international debates and national government responsiveness on ways to counter Gender-Based Violence Against Women (GBVAW) is the question that has mostly influenced this book's research project in its aims and scope. The book is the result of my doctoral dissertation and years of research spent on uncovering policy changes and narratives when debating GBVAW. This research started at the end of 2018 when I won my doctoral fellowship at the LUMSA University in Rome and began to approach the phenomenon. I was firstly fascinated by the idea that, like many concepts in social sciences, violence is an extremely contested notion and idea; violence perpetrated against women is no exception. During the years that have led to this book, I had the chance to share ideas about concepts, definitions, policies, and best practices on the issue. I hope this book will serve the aim of informing people and scholars who want to read the main documents, laws, and policies on GBVAW, understand the best practices, and foresee any new practices to counter GBVAW occurrences.

The fight against violence toward women and gender violence is an increasingly studied and publicly debated social issue. Nevertheless, framing women's rights as human rights remains a fragile terrain globally. The 1995 Beijing declarations, for example, are constantly subjected to a multitude of ongoing political scenarios at all levels, international, regional, and national. More recent international documents and policies have attempted to bridge the gap between the demands of civil society and the understanding of governments and policymakers. However, the responses have varied based on the specific regions of the world, along with the rooted social and cultural aspects of the single countries.

During the years of this research, I have concluded that individuals must have the courage to disrupt an order that does not define – and does not satisfy, at least not anymore – the claims of reality and contemporaneity. Especially after reading the documents individually and conducting the interviews, I realized that the underlying problem of the continued lack of adequate measures to counter GBVAW is the lack of awareness by policymakers of the actual situation of women suffering different forms of violence. This lack of awareness results in either the absence of, or the mistranslation of, declarations of intent and international documents into laws, policy practices, and measures that give women a voice, as its most direct and dramatic consequence.

Even if the experience of laws and policies capable of eliminating and preventing any form of violence against women differs in the various region of the world, the language and, more precisely, the polysemy of words that link violence as an act – and series of acts – to the plural subject of women need to be analyzed in their complexity: in the dialogue between institutions, organizations, movements, and individuals, so as to be able to give timely and shared responses that eradicate a cultural practice from our lives and societies.

Taking into consideration the gravity of the issue, Gender-Based Violence Against Women stands as a critical and contemporary problem deeply entrenched in the cultural mindset and historical context of societies worldwide. By studying this phenomenon and aiming to awaken the conscience of individuals and societies alike, we embark upon a journey that seeks to comprehend why it is presented and perceived in a certain manner rather than another. However, it is important to recognize that this is merely the initial step towards enacting explicit laws and policies that comprehensively safeguard against all forms of violence. It also paves the way for the establishment of a comprehensive European and international legal framework, which unequivocally addresses GBVAW without permitting any exceptions or withdrawal clauses, as observed in certain EU Member States. Above all, it serves as a poignant reminder that women's rights and their entitlement to exist in a world free from violence are fundamental human rights that must never be silenced or disregarded again.

The general objective of this book is to understand how the international and regional documents on GBVAW, and the language and terminology used in the evolution of its global narratives, have influenced the promotion and development of national laws and policies from 1993 to 2015. The research gives special attention to a comparative analysis between Spain and Italy. Spain and Italy are both southern European countries that are part of the traditional model, where men are the primary breadwinners, and women provide secondary income and take care of household duties (Ferrera, 1996, 2005; Barbieri et al., 2015). In terms of gender development and inequality, Spain and Italy rank 25th and 29th, respectively, out of 62 nations with "extremely high human development," according to the Gender Development Index and Gender Inequality Index. However, they are ranked 6th and 14th, respectively, in the 2023 EIGE Gender Equality Index. These countries are often considered similar because of their social and public policy choices (Montoya, 2013). However, they differ significantly in terms of their government responsiveness and ability to address Gender-Based Violence Against Women (Htun & Weldon, 2012). The main focus of this book is to describe and analyze the situation within the territories of Italy and Spain and then compare their experiences and approaches to addressing GBVAW from 1993 to 2015. As a constant thread, so as to propose a comprehensive exploration of the phenomenon, the investigation also considers the reaction and influence of civil society in fighting and preventing GBVAW, with in-depth interviews serving this aim.

Starting with the UN Resolution 48/104 of 1993, the book carefully reconstructs and qualitatively analyzes the documents of the United Nations, the Council of Europe, and the European Union, which have marked policies to prevent and eliminate GBVAW. This creates a fundamental initial overview that leads to understanding the diversity between reactions, laws, and public policies in the two case studies. Within the final objective, this book, thanks to the tools of comparative analysis, interviews, and process tracing, furthers the understanding of the main characteristics that have generated changes among laws and policies on GBVAW in Spain and Italy, within and beyond their differences and similarities.

Chapter I introduces the aims and research questions of this book. Then it draws on the role of international bodies and governments in dealing with GBVAW in literature, presents the primary definition used in the book, and finally outlines the theoretical framework.

Chapter II previews the structure of the book and gives particular attention to the methodology and single methods chosen to answer the research questions. It provides detailed information on the choices behind methodology and methods, as well as the limitations and biases that the research might have encountered.

Chapter III presents the evolution of the main UN, CoE, and EU documents on the issue, focusing on the reference categories and approaches chosen by the different international bodies and organizations from 1993 to 2015. Finally, the chapter shows the importance of framing specific social issues and argues that the way the phenomenon has been framed has either hampered, fostered, or had no effect in creating policy measures. This is developed and discussed in detail in Chapter IV, when the book deals with the comparison between the cases of Italy and Spain.

Chapter IV chronologically shows the development of the laws and policies on GBVAW as adopted in Italy and Spain by using the tools of process tracing (Collier, 2011).

Chapter V, before the conclusions, compares the two cases, using interviews with targeted individuals and the visual representation of policy evolution that allows for the comparison between the two countries of the Northern Mediterranean shore.

The results show that language is a powerful tool to change laws and policies on GBVAW and the reality of societies behind it, but it is also a place of struggle. Furthermore, they elucidate how explicit legislation is critical in establishing rights for women and that collectives, organizations, movements, and other social groups frame countries' historical paths, being a push to some countries and a fundamental supporting tool for others. Finally, social norms, legal aspects, and policy formulations change owing to the dialogue between the civil society and institutional level. Moreover, while highlighting the differences and similarities between the two countries, this book's comparative study points out that both transnational advocacy and organizations are crucial players in fostering changes in the level of government responsiveness to GBVAW.

Chapter I

Gender-Based Violence Against Women: concepts, literature, and background information

Summary: The first chapter of this book presents the main literature the research draws upon, concepts and definitions of the whole book, the theoretical framework it adopts by focusing on the importance of the expressions used to define the phenomenon of GBVAW and the role of international bodies and national governments in producing VAW and GBVAW policy changes. This chapter highlights despite how it might seem quite unpretentious to frame women's rights as human rights, intended as discrimination towards one specific section of society as a violation of multiple human rights, it is still worth mentioning the gender connotation. It expresses how women have been discriminated due to their gender (Ngozi Adichie, 2014). Omitting the word gender in the definition of Violence Against Women would lead to undermining the fact that women have been discriminated and have suffered different forms of violence precisely because of their gender identification.

Introduction

Gender-Based Violence Against Women (GBVAW) is a deeply rooted social issue. Over the last thirty years, it has generated numerous debates and been defined in various ways by the academic community (Walby, 1990; Heise, 1998; Casique & Furegato, 2006; Taylor & Jasinski, 2011), as well as the international community and its various bodies.

The United Nations (UN), the Council of Europe (CoE), and the European Union (EU) have been very attentive to fostering the debate on GBVAW as well as including policies to fight and prevent it (Donato, 2019, 2020). In 1948, the World Health Organization (WHO) constitutional act preamble contained a clear definition of health that would have served the aim of countering GBVAW, "a state of complete physical, mental and social wellbeing and not merely the absence of disease or infirmity." Subsequently, in 1975 the UN began celebrating International Women's Day. However, it was not until the early 1990s that awareness of GBVAW increased in all parts of the world. Since then, the international community has progressively developed a wide range of documents and declarations that have led to regional and national policies to end GBVAW. In 1995, the UN declared that "women's rights are human rights" (Art.14, Beijing Declaration, 1995), thus inserting GBVAW into a debate that considers it to be a set of discriminatory practices. The 1995 Beijing Conference represented one of the momentous events that reflected on women in society and provided for multiple contexts, including social, economic, and religious realities, as well as emphasized the sphere of human rights when debating international policies to contrast GBVAW (Bunch & Carrillo, 1991; Bodelón, 2013; Swanton, 2019). The platform, which was produced as a result of the meeting in China, expresses the will of the international community – represented by national governments' delegations, women's associations, and NGOs who took part in the parallel sessions of discussion at the forum on women in Huairou – to "ensure the full exercise by women and girls of all human rights and to take effective action against violations of these rights, and freedoms" (Article 23, Beijing Declaration, 1995).

In 1995, conceiving GBVAW as a human rights problem opened the debate, both within movements and governments, on acting to 'respond' to the demands of civil society (Weldon, 2006). In 1993, the issue of Male Violence perpetrated Against Women became public knowledge and was therefore a public issue, regardless of the place where it occurs, be it of public or private life (Article 1, 1993 Vienna Declaration, UN/GA 48/104). At the UN level, it was only because of the platform of Beijing that the international community collectively recognized GBVAW as an obstacle to women's rights, freedoms, and personal development and inserted it in the framework of gender mainstreaming that in 1999 also led to the creation of the International Day for the Elimination of Violence Against Women on November 25.[1]

Subsequently, in collaboration with the UN, the Council of Europe (CoE) – a sub-regional organization between the international UN and the regional European Union (EU) – dealt with GBVAW with the Istanbul Convention in 2011. At a lower level, the EU signed the 2011 Istanbul Convention and fostered both a soft law and binding documents to its Member States (Walby, 2004; Roth, 2008; Montoya, 2013). The way these international bodies have addressed GBVAW has been crucial to both the degree of Government Responsiveness in terms of policies (Htun & Weldon, 2012) and the way social movements have mobilized in different areas of the world (Weldon, 2006).

---

[1] The day was chosen to honor the Mirabal sisters who – because of their political activism – were brutally killed in 1961 by the Dominican dictator Rafael Trujillo.

Moreover, the rejection of the unequal status of women in societies and the effective condemnation of GBVAW as a form of discrimination (EIGE, 2021) – established by international declarations and documents of the UN, CoE, and EU – have proved to be of crucial importance. These declarations and intentions have emphasized how the language and the choice of specific words used to address this social problem have extremely deep cultural and linguistic roots (Eastel et al., 2012; Corradi & Donato, 2019) and how they play a fundamental role in disciplining both the regulations and political strategies to address the fight against GBVAW.

Research questions and research goal

In light of the growing importance of GBVAW as a global issue over the past three decades, the research goal of this book is to understand how international (UN, CoE) and regional (EU) documents on GBVAW, as well as the specific language and choice of specific words in the documents (Eastel et al., 2012), have contributed to different policy responses in fighting and preventing GBVAW in Italy and Spain. Starting with a top-down approach, from the analysis of the UN, CoE, and EU documents to Italian and Spanish laws and policies, this book also considers the reaction and influence of civil society in contrasting GBVAW, with the aim of proposing a comprehensive study of the phenomenon in a comparative perspective, also using in-depth semi-structured interviews (Horton et al., 2004) with targeted individuals. The interviewees were people who identified as women and men who dealt with policies on GBVAW. In detail, I carried out interviews with a) activists in movements and organizations; b) NGOs leaders and members; c) members of national and international institutions that work on GBVAW; d) researchers that work on GBVAW.

Finally, to reach the frame and content of the research goal, the book formulates the following Research Questions (RQs):

RQ1: What were the most relevant international documents on GBVAW over the period 1993-2015? (In terms of how they were important for single EU nation-states (Italy and Spain), definitions and categories of analysis, binding measures, moral suasion)

RQ2: In Spain and Italy, which factors produced a different reception of international and regional documents within the national laws and systems of policies?

RQ3: Why and how have the two countries on the northern shore of the Mediterranean responded differently to GBVAW (focusing on the first step in policy-making: government responsiveness)?

In the following paragraphs, I will briefly present the most relevant literature on the role of governments in contrasting GBVAW, theories of Violence perpetrated by Men Against Women, the main concepts used in this book, and, finally, I will move to the conclusions of this chapter.

The role of international bodies and governments in dealing with GBVAW in current literature: laws, policies, and government responsiveness

This book draws upon the most relevant studies on the social issue. These studies are of crucial relevance as they will assist to later analyzing, discussing, and comparing documents by the international organizations and policies adopted by nation-states from 1993 to 2015 to contrast GBVAW, with a specific focus on Italy and Spain.

In a cross-national analysis of policies, Corradi and Stöckl (2016) adopt a historical perspective and identify those actors that play a role in the fight against GBVAW, or VAW, as in the article, namely: the state, social movements, and supra-national bodies. They concentrate on VAW policy regimes and the role of the state in fighting VAW and suggest that the state is a strong, powerful actor in the fight against VAW, but only if it works "under the pressure from or in combination with both independent social movements and supra-national bodies" (p.14). Moreover, the historical paths of individual countries and social movements are fundamental drivers of policy change concerning VAW. This is quite clear in the differences between Italy and Spain on VAW policies. Corradi and Stöckl consider Spain as an intermediate country in the development of VAW policies where governmental action started between the late 1980s and early 1990s, right after the end of the Francoist dictatorship[2] , and has increased since then. Whereas Italy is a relatively newcomer country, meaning that public support for combatting VAW has existed only since the mid-1990s due to the lack of dialogue between the state and social movements. They also highlight the role of the EU as an accelerator for change, but only in respect of services to women and more coordinated interventions, namely ex-post strategies to counter VAW. They highlight the poor capacity of the EU to foresee preventive strategies to contrast VAW occurrences.

Montoya (2013) asserts that for domestic policies to change international and regional changes are vitally important. However, the author suggests that there should be an emphasis on how to connect the global to the local for tools and strategies to be effective. Montoya, as well as Weldon and Htun (2013), addresses the role of transnational advocacy in improving opportunities for change at the local level to contrast Violence Against Women. For example, the EU, says

---

[2] The Francoist dictatorship lasted for 36 years from 1939 to 1975.

Montoya (2013), works on VAW in mainly 3 ways: norm dissemination, coercion, and capacity building. Montoya invites us to look "beyond rhetorical legal changes to examine the ways international organizations might impact domestic practices" (p. 3). This also means looking outside the context of national government policy to understand how international and regional organizations, as well as transnational networks, can bring about change on these issues, including by connecting with advocates and local realities.

In Htun and Weldon's work (2012), VAW is conceptualized as a violation of human rights and an important concern for social policy. These two brilliant authors demonstrate how autonomous movements produce an enduring impact on VAW policy through the institutionalization of feminist ideas in international norms. Htun and Weldon (2012) use panel data from 70 countries and conclude that "the most important and consistent factor driving policy change is feminist activism" (p. 231). They also add that local and domestic activism and movements interact with national, regional, and international organizations and networks to influence policy-making. Their research highlights the role of autonomous feminist movements for VAW policy change (as in Weldon, 2002) by defining them as "a form of women's mobilization that is devoted to promoting women's status and wellbeing independently of political and other associations that do not have the status of women as their main concern" (p. 553). In their study, the concept of transnational advocacy by feminist movements is of pivotal importance since the latter have the capacity to magnify the effects of international treaties by making explicit the differences between ratifying and implementing such treaties. VAW policies, framed as a social progressive set of policies, create and replicate a specific normative and social order, and aim to improve the status and opportunities of women, seen as vulnerable and disadvantaged parts of the societies. For VAW policies to be effective, the authors assert that autonomous social movements are essential "to catalyze the process of progressive social policy change and its continuation" in order to challenge the fact that "VAW is ubiquitous" (p. 549). They adopt a specific Index of Government Responsiveness (GR) – the intensity of policy adoption by governments – to VAW in order to compare how states responded to VAW as a social issue. The index contains a maximum of 10 points, divided as follows: 1) Three points for services to victims: Government funds domestic violence shelters; Government funds rape crisis centers; Government provides crisis services for other forms of violence; 2) Three points for legal reform: Government has adopted specialized legislation pertaining to domestic violence; Government has adopted specialized legislation pertaining to sexual assault/rape; Government has adopted specialized legalization pertaining to other forms of violence; 3) One point for policies or programs targeted at vulnerable populations of women: Government provides specialized services to women of marginalized groups; Government recognizes violence against women as a basis for refugee status; Government protects immigrant women in abusive relations from deportation; 4) One point for training professionals who respond to victims: Government provides training for police, social workers, nurses, etc.; 5) One point for prevention programs: Government funds public education programs or takes other preventive measures; 6) One point for administrative reforms: Government maintains specialized agency to provide leadership, coordination, and support for VAW policies across different sectors and levels. (p. 550-551). In the specific case of Italy and Spain, they calculate that the VAW government responsiveness index is always rated 0 in Italy, except in the last year they consider, in 2005, when it is assessed as 3, while in Spain it is 0 in 1975 but then quickly increases from 1 to 5 (Ibid., Annex A).

In a later work, Weldon and Htun (2013) declare that any laws and legal reforms should specifically mention that Violence Against Women is a crime and that feminist movements in collaboration with political movements have the potential to mobilize citizens while also prioritizing the agenda of governments and institutions to generate government responsiveness on the issue.

McBride et al. (2010) concentrate on the pivotal collaboration between women's movements and women's policy agency in policy-making and make use of the definition of state feminism: state action and policy outcomes follow feminist ideas with the final aim of promoting gender equality and women's inclusion in the political arena. The authors define women's policy agencies as state-based agencies that are both established by government statute or decree, with the aim of promoting sex-based equality and the improvement of women's status (p. 29), and women's movement as social movements interested in the promotion of women's interests. The authors present a cross-national comparison of 13 countries and consider both the cases of Italy and Spain, part of the comparison section presented in chapter four of this book. They argue that from the mid-1980s through to 2002, Spain did not develop any form of state feminism, whereas Italy "ranks among the countries with the highest successes" in the Southern European Catholic countries (p. 98). However, in McBride's et al. analysis, there is no reference to specific VAW policies, and the period analyzed in Spain ended in 2002, before the socialist presidency of Zapatero (2004-2011), who brought about social and feminist policy changes in the country. In her analysis of the different patterns and strategies of reform in the field of VAW policies, Montoya (2013) also refers to state feminism. She defines "reform" as the domestic policy change on VAW that results from the action of global institutions and movements, identifying four ways to VAW policy reforms: domestically driven reform (strong domestic advocates and government responsiveness), transnationally driven reform (interaction between international and domestic advocates), internationally driven reform (interaction between an international organization and the state), and no reform (p. 27).

Roggeband (2012) highlights the differences in nation-states with reference to specific policies aimed at contrasting domestic Violence Against Women. The author analyses two countries from a comparative perspective: Spain and the Netherlands. The study pays specific attention to the vital role of "frame negotiation, left-wing governments, and strong feminist mobilization" in addressing domestic VAW. The article looks at the interactions between the state and women's movements in the two countries over three decades. It concludes that the interaction among parties in governments, feminist mobilizations, and the way the issue is framed changes the extent of this typology of progressive policy. For example, Spain "has become a vanguard country in this policy domain by introducing a comprehensive law against gendered violence" (p. 758) precisely because of the interplay of different actors on the scene: women's movements and machineries, among others.

Kantola (2006) analyses the role of governments, parliaments, and women's movements as an instrument of change for VAW policies, adopting a feminist perspective and comparing the cases of Britain and Finland. She focuses on how feminists engage with the state, how their discourses construct the state, and how all this influences social change. She also refers to the EU as an important actor in synthesizing discourses between the Member States and other international organizations. She points out the differences in policies and responses to domestic violence by highlighting the embedded feminist discourses in the two countries.

Swanton (2019) highlights the role of the media as a sounding board for GBVAW/VAW, representing it as a threat to the social order, rather than only to its victims. They also have the power to set the agenda of governments and, therefore, induce some policy change on the issue.

Feci and Schettini (2017) examine the different chronological stages of the evolution of VAW/GBVAW rights and policies in Italy. The authors state that 1975 was a crucial turning point in the country's attention to VAW. Specifically, one event that triggered the attention of the media, and to a considerable extent, of the whole civil society on the issue: it is the Circeo case.[3] The crime was committed by three young men belonging to wealthy families in the Italian capital (p. 173), resulting in the death of one and the suffering of the memory and violations suffered by the other. The two young women did not belong to

---

[3] The Circeo case or massacre is a case of kidnapping and murder that occurred in the Italian municipality of San Felice Circeo, on the Pontine coast, in the promontory of the same name on the Tyrrhenian Sea, not far from Rome, between 29 and 30 September 1975. The victims were two young women, Donatella Colasanti and Rosaria Lopez, who were raped, butchered, and tortured by Gianni Guido, Angelo Izzo and Andrea Ghira. Lopez died because of the violence and torture suffered.

the same class as their abusers. The evident implications of this tremendous episode in the life of the young democratic country were and continue to be of considerable significance. Italians were no longer faced with the notion that Violence Against Women was a phenomenon to be relegated to the less advantaged classes of society, who are faced with problems of an economic nature and who react in an abrupt manner to behavior they do not accept from their partner. In the late 1970s, Violence Against Women extended from the domestic setting to the non-demarcated space that encompasses private life but that overlooks and spreads to the public sphere. As in Feci and Schettini's book, it is crucial to remember how in that period, sexual violence, from the norms of the Rocco code in Italy, was violence committed not against the person but against the public morals. In the years that followed the massacre, a new feminist awareness emerged, and both rape and domestic violence became political issues. Due to this event, women started to denounce the silence that – for so long – had accompanied crimes perpetrated against women, the role of the police in dissuading women from making a complaint, the transformation of the raped woman from the accuser and injured party into the accused (Feci & Schettini, 2017, p.180). For example, in the same years, the lawyer Tina Langostena Bassi launched a popular initiative against violence against women and the abolition of shotgun marriages. A 24/7 domestic violence hotline was demanded, without any success. Nevertheless, the resonance of the event and the protests that ensued were so high in Italy that there was a call for a popular Italian legislative initiative towards a law that could transform the crime of rape into a crime against the person and not against morals. Feminists from different countries decided to hold a meeting in Rome with the proposal of an international court against rape. However, it was only with Law 66/1996 that Italy sanctioned the passage from a conception of physical violence as a crime against morality to a crime against the person. In their research, Feci and Schettini (2017) also refer to the crucial role of the EU in the process of developing VAW/GBVAW policies and rights. For example, in 1984, Heide D'Ancona in the European Parliament (EP) proposed the Feminist Report on the situation in member countries concerning GBVAW/VAW. The Amsterdam Treaty of 1997-99 established the principle of gender mainstreaming. The authors highlight an interesting aspect in reference to the way the EU referred to VAW in those years: by only voicing it aloud in public health contexts. However, some of the female Members of the EU Parliament (MEPs) expressed their disagreement on this since, according to them, it was not a mere threat to health but specified that the concept of the well-being of the individual had to be broadened as to comprehensively account for the violation of fundamental rights and the principle of equality. In 1997, the European Parliament (EP) approved the first European campaign on zero tolerance with respect to VAW/GBVAW, with transnational projects co-financed by Women

Against Violence Europe (WAVE)[4] and the beginning of a constant lobbying action at the European institutions by feminist advocates. The Daphne program – now part of the more general program Rights, Equality, and Citizenship (2014-2020) – was created in 1999, which includes the aim of eliminating GBVAW as a violation of fundamental rights (p. 220). With Directive 2006/54/EC, "for the first time in a binding legislation, sexual harassment in the workplace is indicated as punishable in the same way as any other discrimination on the basis of sex" (p. 214). They are interesting aspects that influenced how Italy responded to VAW/GBVAW and the effect that international and regional organizations, together with the central state, had in producing policy changes on the issue.

Valiente (2002) concentrates on the case of Spain and analyses the evolution of VAW inside the country: state legislations, policies, women's movements, and services. The author highlights the main historical moments that overturned the perceptions of VAW, therefore, ways to counter its occurrences, starting with the end of the Francoist dictatorship in 1975. She concludes that the problem with effective policies to contrast VAW is the implementation phase. This happens mostly because people in charge of policy implementation are often men who do not want to challenge or jeopardize their position. She also argues that feminists "need to put pressure on the behavior of institutional actors not only to get them to continue to develop new measures against violence but also to ensure that they implement existing measures much more effectively" (Valiente, 2002, p. 121) and that the collaboration between civil society, professionals, non-governmental actors, and institutions is of paramount importance to achieve new policies better suited to counteracting violence. This has proven to be true, especially in more recent times, beginning with the first Zapatero government and up to the present years, with different takes, where the enabling factor has been the sharing of decisions between parties within the Spanish parliament, with pressure from women's movements and agencies (such as the Women's Institute), academics, and party activists (García, 2016). The most relevant example of good collaboration, dialogue, and compromise between the PSOE, PP, and feminist and women's organizations was the adoption of the 2004 'Organic Law on integrated protective measures against Gender Violence' (VioGen). A law that responded to the main demands of civil society, of the left-wing movements, feminist and social movements and was approved unanimously by the Spanish parliament respecting – to some extent – a gender perspective on the issue as at the EU level (Lombardo & Rolandsen Agustín, 2016).

---

[4] For more information check this website: https://wave-network.org/.

Della Porta (2003) considers the interplay between women's organizations and institutions, be they of the central of local authorities, to produce policy changes. In Italy, Della Porta claims that – especially in the 1990s – women's movements tried to pressure the state into their political struggles being heard but had mostly failed to enter – or willingly preferred – not to be in the political games of the central government. Consequently, it has excluded some of the real possibilities of bringing their demands to the higher powers (Parliament) and fighting for women's rights, including the right to live a life free from violence.

Furthermore, feminist theory has been instrumental in understanding the root causes of Gender-Based Violence Against Women. According to Conway (2016), a theory on violence that is gender-blind and without a feminist lens inevitably results in the presentation of the dominant patriarchal perspective. Feminist theories examining gender-specific violence tend to remain within the confines of the male-female binary (Heyes, 2013). However, if the feminist lens is to offer a complete understanding of violence on the global stage, the feminist space needs to be opened up to include the analysis of violence in a more comprehensive way and include people who identify with different genders (Heyes, 2013).

Feminist theorists assert that gender-based violence in armed conflict is primarily based on and perpetuated by patriarchy and heterosexual masculine norms (Kinyanda et al., 2017). Feminist theory maintains that women's violence stems from their victimization and oppressive experiences as women and mothers (Bourassa & Bertrand, 2018).

In existing Theoretical Work on the Relationship between Feminist Theory and the Democratic Regime, Pateman (1988) argues that democracy is inherently patriarchal and exclusionary towards women. He argues that the democratic regime, while promoting equality in theory, often fails to address power imbalances and gender hierarchies. Fraser (1990) contends that liberal feminism's focus on equal rights fails to address systemic inequalities. Maron Young (2000) argues that democratic theory must be reimagined to include marginalized groups such as women. Young also highlights the significance of intersectionality in understanding and addressing violence against women, emphasizing the need to consider multiple forms of oppression. Verloo (2005) argues for policy measures and institutional reforms that aim to challenge the underlying power structures perpetuating gender-based violence. Developing prevention programs, providing accessible support services, and engaging men and boys as allies have also been identified as important strategies (Jewkes et al., 2015; WHO, 2013). Hence, feminist theories have significantly contributed to the understanding of Gender-Based Violence Against Women and its relationship with the democratic regime. In this book, I will examine how democratic life and changes in the governments have had an influence on government responsiveness towards GBVAW. For instance, in 1975, after the death of the Spanish dictator Francisco Franco GBVAW GR accelerated, while in Italy, democratic life since 1978 did not impact policy formation on GBVAW (Corradi & Donato, 2023). In this strand of studies, Pateman (1988) critically examines the democratic theory, highlighting the exclusion of women's voices and experiences from the public sphere. Fraser (2009) expands on this critique, arguing that democratic regimes often fail to address the economic, social, and cultural dimensions of gender inequality. Maron Young (2000) focuses on the concept of political responsibility, emphasizing the need for a democratic regime that holds institutions accountable for addressing gender-based violence. Verloo (2005) explores the intersection of feminist theory and democratic governance, advocating for policies that challenge the structural roots of violence against women.

Gender-Based Violence Against Women (GBVAW) continues to be a pressing societal issue, prompting researchers to explore the interconnectedness of various authors' perspectives on the subject. This literature review delves into the linkages between GBVAW and Violence Against Women (VAW) policies, emphasizing the vital role of dialogue between national governments, feminist movements, and women's organizations to achieve government responsiveness and foster policy formation. It further contends that while democratic life is crucial, additional factors are necessary to foster comprehensive policy formation in this critical domain.

The debate on definitions:
literature concerning violence perpetrated by men against women

The concept of Violence perpetrated Against Women is part of a broad debate that has generated plenty of definitions and approaches. However, over the last few decades, there are two main paradigms on which current literature has been arguing: Violence Against Women (VAW) and Gender Violence (GV).

Gender Violence considers male domination and patriarchy over women as the most relevant problems that lead to violence because women inside the society still occupy a position of inferiority (Merry, 2009; Taylor & Jasinski, 2011). Gender Violence is, therefore, "a critical theoretical category that constitutes and is constitutional by power relationships" (Nayak & Suchland, 2006, p. 4). Sexual, physical, and psychological violence that functions through gender constructs and is frequently at the nexus of sexuality, race, and national identity is referred to as gender violence.

Violence Against Women, the second paradigm, develops in an ecological model (Casique & Furegato, 2006) and acknowledges diverse, intersecting dimensions among personal, situational, and sociocultural factors (Heise,

1998, p. 263). The individual or personal level refers to the dialogue inside the couple – or the two main individuals involved in the violent situation. The relational level relates to known environmental dynamics concerning friends and family, which might prevent or foster violent behaviors. The relational level considers the broader level of society and the prevalent culture it possesses.

There are multiple other ways in which the phenomenon has been framed (Walby et al., 2017), such as Male Violence Against Women (MVAW), an expression that has 'fortune' since it enables to indicate both the aggressor and the victim in some studies, for example, Flood (2011) and Ciccone (2017), but also Violencia(s) machista(s). This expression has found its success, especially in Spanish-speaking territories, in both its singular and plural forms, which denotes the impossibility of separating the various forms of violence from the physical to the psychological, economic, and symbolic – to epitomize the structural shape and diffusion in the cultural mindset of societies, where the patriarchal order is identified as the culprit, capable of generating multiple forms of violence, called "las violencias machistas" (González, 2012).

Gender-Based Violence Against Women (GBVAW), as in Baker and Leicht (2017), focuses on the cultural roots of violence as historically perpetrated by one group of society (men) against the other (women) because of the unbalance of gender power. They see the contradictions that a globalized and more interconnected world might imply and is implying, for both men and women, in terms of how states deal with GBVAW, but at the same time, insist on how changes in gender roles, as they are evolving in current times, and in the social and economic status of men and women in society, are the key elements to consider when creating policies to counter GBVAW. In other words, on the basis of this type of violence, there is a difference in terms of gender status that, on the one hand, is a cause of the violence itself and, on the other, is the consequence of a lack of solution. It is the same binary division in terms of roles (man versus woman); for this reason, "Against Women," as a cultural heritage of all societies – with the appropriate differences for areas of the world – which prevents the dismantling of the patriarchal structure in both the domestic and political sphere. At the same time, this awareness is at the heart of the deconstruction of GBVAW, which remains a widespread cultural problem with extraordinarily strong roots.

However, even though many debates have populated the discussion on this specific section of socially progressive policies, the two main paradigms of GV and VAW still lead the international arena. For the purpose of this book, I chose to use Gender-Based Violence Against Women since I assume it addresses both the main causes of violence, linked to differences inside the societies and the gender constructs that exist at the international as well as nation-states level, but also encompasses the ecological approach of VAW. Furthermore, this expression is becoming more familiar at the global level and, together with

Male Violence Against Women, I believe it could help frame the issue in both preventing and contrasting its occurrences, more than describing what it is all about.

Additionally, the concept of masculine dominance is determinant to understanding how GBVAW has been a structural condition of women's lives in different ages and contexts. Bourdieu discussed the topic of symbolic violence and referred it to that typology of violence that is "symbolic, sweet, insensitive, invisible for the victims themselves, which is exercised essentially through the purely symbolic ways of communication and knowledge, more precisely, misknowledge, recognition, and gratitude or, at the limit, sentiment" (Bourdieu, 2001, p. 8).[5] This type of violence is visible in the documents of the international organizations that are discussed in this book, especially those of the CoE, and therefore, remains crucial to mention in the theoretical framework. According to Bourdieu, symbolic violence is the most insidious form of VAW since it is exercised by the dominator (men), who imposes a certain vision of the world on the dominated (women). Since symbolic violence is related to power and dominance, it reproduces itself in different sites by engaging apparatuses, strategies, and mechanisms of control (Hooks, 1999). This is reminiscent, in part, of the way Foucault understood domination in terms of power relations that control and admonish.

This asserted Bourdieu is not inevitable (p.16): the order can change, and the social vision and division can be eluded.

On a global scale, contemporary society women's movements, civil society, and activists of the new wave of feminism – those who share the claims of the NiUnaMenos movement born in Argentina[6] and the American #Me Too[7] – are asking the international community and their national governments to be more

---

[5] In Italian: "simbolica, dolce, insensibile, invisibile per le stesse vittime che si esercita essenzialmente attraverso le vie puramente simboliche della comunicazione e della conoscenza, più precisamente, della mis-conoscenza, del riconoscimento e della riconoscenza o, al limite, del sentimento."

[6] A Latin American fourth-wave grassroots feminist movement, active since 2015 and specifically focuses on GBVAW.

The fourth wave of feminism began roughly in 2012 – although not everyone agrees on its existence – it has a focus on sexual harassment, body shaming, and rape culture, among other issues. The use of social media is crucial within the fourth wave and is used by activists to highlight and address issues related to women's empowerment, gender rights and gender violence.

[7] North American social movement who fights against sexual abuse and sexual harassment and it is active since 2006. It has become viral since October 2017 when there were several sexual-abuse allegations against film producer Harvey Weinstein.

responsive to address the fight against Gender-Based Violence comprehensively and to challenge the structure of gender relationships. Consequently, groups of women and men have started and continue to fight against vulnerability and believe that they are equal to men and men are – willingly or not – going to deal with this new balance of power (York, 2011). Most social scientists agree that Gender-Based Violence in domestic environments is highly correlated with the stress of gender relations in which men persistently try to maintain their male authority and do not challenge the paradoxical character of the doxa (Bourdieu, 2001; Burt, 1980). It is often the case that women do not report abuse for fear of rejection by their families or exposure to further violence. On the other hand, the institutional tolerance of domestic violence fuels a culture of impunity that contributes to normalizing violence (Federici, 2018). Moreover, perpetrating violence – ranging from physical and emotional violence to psychological assaults, homicide, and sexual assaults – exacerbates conservative gender roles built on man's superiority and increases the sense of vulnerability and weakness in women who are abused and feel trapped (Adler, 2003; York, 2011).

Gender-Based Violence Against Women is a practice of discrimination that needs to be urgently addressed on various levels (Cimagalli, 2014).

> "Violence matters. It wrecks lives. It causes injury and misery. Violence is both a cause and consequence of inequality. It is a violation of human rights. Violence is a detriment to health and to sustainable economic development. Ending violence would be a major contribution to human wellbeing. A life free from violence is much valued. Preventing violence is a widely shared goal." (Walby et al., 2017, p. 1)

In "The concept and measurement of violence against women and men," Walby et al. (2017) focus on how despite VAW is still a consequence of gender inequality, most statistics, especially national and official ones, render it invisible, leading to a dichotomy of "gender invisibility/no gender" and/ or "women only." Therefore, GBVAW needs to be holistically envisioned to put forward practices at a national and international level capable of contrasting this cultural social issue by also rethinking the concept and practices of masculinity.

Additional definitions for the book

Other important definitions for this book refer to the state and its role in producing GBVAW policies and are presented as follows.

State is an entity endowed with territorial political power, exercising such power in its original capacity over a specific territory and people, in a constant and active way and in full independence from other entities.

Government is the executive branch of the entire administrative apparatus, which is responsible for the concrete realization of the goals of the state, mostly determined in terms of laws and policies.

Laws are any prescription that constitutes an element of the legal system. In the specific case of national laws approved by the Parliament, a law is a legal act enacted by the bodies to which the State Constitution attributes legislative power.

Policy/policies comprise different measures taken by governments to address a specific political issue, such as national plans, but also international and regional programs as transposed into specific states' laws and policies.

GBVAW policies are those public policies that aim to counter GBVAW, be they at the international, regional, or national levels.

A UN resolution refers to a formal decision or recommendation adopted by the United Nations (UN) General Assembly, Security Council, or other specialized UN bodies. Resolutions are key instruments through which the UN addresses global issues, sets forth principles, and outlines actions to be taken by member states and the international community. They serve as authoritative statements of the UN's position and intentions on a particular matter. UN resolutions are non-binding. They express the opinion or recommendations of the UN, urging member states to take certain actions or adhere to specific principles. While non-binding, these resolutions hold significant moral and political weight, often shaping the global discourse and influencing national policies on specific issues.

A UN report refers to a document prepared by the United Nations to provide information, analysis, and recommendations on a specific issue or topic. Reports are produced by UN specialized agencies, programs, and other bodies to document and disseminate findings, progress, challenges, and proposals related to their respective mandates. UN reports are not legally binding documents but carry significant weight in shaping policy decisions and informing international discourse. They serve as authoritative sources of information, analysis, and expertise, providing valuable insights into global challenges and potential solutions. UN reports are used by member states, civil society organizations, researchers, and policymakers to guide decision-making processes, advocate for change, and promote international cooperation. They contribute to raising awareness, identifying best practices, and fostering dialogue on critical global issues. While UN reports do not have direct enforcement mechanisms, their influence stems from the credibility and expertise of the UN as an international organization. Governments and stakeholders often take into account the findings and recommendations of UN reports when formulating policies, implementing programs, and seeking solutions to complex global problems.

An EU directive is a legal instrument issued by the European Union (EU) that sets out specific objectives and general principles to be achieved by the member states. Directives are binding on the EU member states concerning the results to be achieved but leave the choice of the form and methods of implementation to the national authorities. They provide a framework for harmonizing laws, regulations, and administrative provisions across EU countries, aiming to ensure consistency and facilitate the functioning of the internal market. Member states are required to adopt national legislation that aligns with the objectives outlined in the directive within a specified timeframe. The monitoring and enforcement of EU resolutions, reports, and directives are carried out through various mechanisms. The European Commission, as the executive body of the EU, plays a crucial role in monitoring the implementation of EU legislation, including resolutions, reports, and directives. It assesses the compliance of member states and takes necessary actions, such as initiating infringement procedures if a member state fails to fulfill its obligations. Additionally, the Court of Justice of the European Union (CJEU) serves as the judicial authority responsible for ensuring the interpretation and application of EU law. Individuals, organizations, or member states can bring cases before the CJEU to seek legal remedies or challenge non-compliance with EU directives or other legal obligations. When an EU directive is adopted, it becomes binding on the member states, which are required to transpose it into their national legal systems. Each member state is responsible for implementing the directive by enacting national laws, regulations, or administrative provisions that align with the objectives and requirements set forth in the directive. The member states typically have a specified period, usually a few years, to complete the transposition process and notify the European Commission of the measures taken. The European Union has adopted various legislative measures to address gender-based violence and promote gender equality. These measures include directives, regulations, and recommendations that establish common standards and guidelines for member states. To enforce legislation related to gender-based violence, member states are expected to take necessary steps to implement and enforce the relevant directives within their national legal frameworks. The European Commission monitors the implementation progress and can initiate infringement procedures against member states that fail to fulfill their obligations.

An EU resolution is a formal decision or statement adopted by the European Union (EU) or one of its institutions, bodies, or agencies. Resolutions are used to express the collective position, intent, or recommendation of the EU on specific issues, policies, or objectives. They serve as guidelines or political statements that aim to shape the EU's stance on a particular matter. EU resolutions can address a wide range of topics, including foreign policy, human rights, economic matters, and other areas of EU competence. Enforcement rules for EU resolutions depend on their nature and the authority of the institution or body issuing them. While EU resolutions are not legally binding, they can have important political implications and serve as a basis for subsequent actions. Here are some key aspects of enforcement related to EU resolutions. They often carry significant political weight and can influence the decision-making processes of EU member states. They shape the policy agenda, guide discussions, and serve as a reference point for future actions at the EU level. In certain cases, EU resolutions may be followed by specific measures or actions that aim to implement the objectives outlined in the resolution. These measures can take various forms, such as the development of policies, programs, guidelines, or recommendations that member states are encouraged to adopt and implement. The European Commission, as the executive body of the EU, typically monitors the implementation of EU resolutions. It assesses the progress made by member states in aligning their policies and actions with the objectives set forth in the resolution. Monitoring can involve regular reporting, data collection, and evaluation of the implementation efforts.EU resolutions can trigger political dialogues and negotiations among EU member states, institutions, and other stakeholders. These discussions aim to facilitate consensus-building, coordination, and cooperation in addressing the issues raised in the resolution. They provide a platform for exchanging views, sharing best practices, and exploring possible joint actions. EU resolutions can exert soft power and influence through diplomatic channels. They can shape the EU's external relations and interactions with other countries, international organizations, or regional entities. EU resolutions can serve as a basis for diplomatic negotiations, advocacy, or raising awareness of specific issues on the international stage. It's important to note that the enforcement of EU resolutions primarily relies on the political will and commitment of member states to implement the recommended actions or policies. While EU institutions can facilitate and monitor the process, the ultimate responsibility for enforcement lies with the individual member states and their national authorities.

Whereas, EU communication refers to the process of disseminating information, engaging with stakeholders, and promoting dialogue within the European Union (EU) and with external audiences. It encompasses the various methods, strategies, and channels used by EU institutions, bodies, and agencies to communicate their policies, initiatives, and decisions to the public, member states, and other stakeholders. EU communication plays a crucial role in promoting transparency, fostering understanding, and ensuring the active participation of citizens in the EU's decision-making processes.

Finally, Government Responsiveness (GR) to GBVAW is the way governments respond to GBVAW in the matter of creating responsive national governmental policies. Some authors (i.e., Htun & Weldon, 2012; Roggeband, 2012) use an index to calculate the level of single states' Government Responsiveness, as in the literature review presented in the previous paragraphs.

Theoretical framework

For the purpose of this book, the description and analysis of the documents of international, regional, and national documents and the comparative analysis between the GBVAW laws and policies in Italy and Spain, the theoretical framework studies the evolution of the definitions and concepts with reference to Violence perpetrated against Women as in the debate between GV, considering authors like Merry (2009), Nayak and Suchland (2006), Taylor and Jasinski (2011), among others, and VAW with reference to Heise (1998) and Casique and Furegato (2006). It looks at the main theoretical categories as presented in the various documents and policies of the international, regional, and national bodies, considering the concept of symbolic violence as in Bourdieu (2001) and, eventually, stresses the novel formulations of the issue as they are emerging in recent laws and policies: GBVAW as briefly presented in Baker and Leicht (2017), MVAW as in Flood (2011) and Ciccone (2017), Violencia(s) Machista(s) as in González (2012) and the implications the use of these expressions has on the preferred strategies for GBVAW laws and policies, especially at the national level.

For the comparative analysis, the main points of reference are the article of Roggeband (2012), Kantola (2006), and Corradi and Stöckl (2016) for both the historical assessment of the differences and similarities between the two countries as in the first two studies, the section on the Spanish context as in Roggeband (2012) and Corradi and Stöckl (2016) – both examining a similar time period in VAW policy analysis as that of this book – and finally, the different actors involved in setting the agenda of governments and producing GBVAW/VAW policy change as discussed in the three studies, and with some reference to the work of Swanton (2019) concerning the power of media to influence the national agenda setting on GBVAW. Historical GBVAW policies in the countries also deal with the analyses of the work of several authors, as in Valiente (2002) on the importance of state feminism and women in positions of legislative and political power to witness changes in VAW policy-making and implementation for the Spanish case, and Feci and Schettini (2017) for the Italian chronological evolution of the laws and policies on VAW/GBVAW, on the differences based on the political powers in charge at different points on history and on the role of the EU in pushing for national laws and policies to become part of the national scenario. However, contrary to the above-mentioned studies, this book focuses on how single GBVAW domestic policies sense the effect of international and regional changes and, therefore, accepts the invitation of Montoya (2013) to draw attention to the role of transnational advocacy to bring about national change on GBVAW policies. The book also considers the collaboration between women's movements and women's policy agencies in comparing the cases of Italy and Spain to see the differences in GBVAW policy responses and to continue the work of McBride et al. (2010) that has no focus on GBVAW, that of Della Porta (2003) on the specific case of Italy and its failures in terms of GBVAW-GR, and the studies of Lombardo and Forest (2015) and Lombardo and Rolandsen Agustín (2016) on the EU and Spanish gender perspective on the matter.

The differences and similarities between VAW policies in different countries and the reference to the index of government responsiveness reflect the studies of Weldon and Htun (2013). However, while previous studies analyzed policy changes in a panel of 70 countries, this book focuses on a narrower comparison between two countries that are often considered comparable and similar with reference to the socially progressive policies they choose to adopt (Ferrara 1996, 2015; Dogan, 2002; Barbieri et al., 2015). This book considers the importance of autonomous movements in both countries as a trigger to GBVAW policy changes but – mostly – unravels the role of international and regional bodies in pressuring for VAW policy changes at the national level. It also highlights the differences in the national parliaments as a historical determinant of how laws and policies on GBVAW evolved differently in Spain and Italy (1993-2015).

Finally, while previous studies have underlined either single states regimes of VAW policy change in specific years or a panel of states, this book starts with the description and analysis of the most relevant international documents on GBVAW in a new, unprecedented work about the theoretical and analytical categories used within the documents, laws, and policies and the specific issues related to GBAW (i.e. domestic violence, sexual harassment, shelters for victims, rehabilitation programs for aggressors, among others) since they characterized the period from 1993 to 2015. This book later focuses on the comparison of two countries of the European Union: Spain and Italy, to highlight the similarities and differences through a chronological analysis of laws and policies and, lastly, through testimonies of participants based on in-depth interviews carried out in Spain and Italy in the original languages.

It is all about gender

This first chapter of this book has provided an overview of the main literature, concepts, and definitions that serve as the foundation for the entire work. It has explored the theoretical framework adopted, with particular emphasis on the significance of the expression used to define the phenomenon of Gender-

Based Violence Against Women (GBVAW), as well as the role of international bodies and national governments in shaping policies addressing Violence Against Women (VAW) and GBVAW. This chapter has highlighted how despite it seeming quite unpretentious to frame women's rights as human rights, intended as discrimination towards one specific section of society as a violation of multiple human rights, the gender connotation is worth mentioning. It expresses how women have been discriminated because of their gender (Ngozi Adichie, 2014). Omitting gender in the definition of Violence Against Women would lead to undermining the fact that women have been discriminated and have suffered different forms of violence precisely because of their gender identification.

All concepts arise in specific contexts, in determined times, but contexts change, and times evolve. Language and the choice of specific words (Eastel et al., 2012; Aksan, 2009) influence people's perceptions, affect the understanding of the phenomenon and contribute to its characterization inside societies (Schapp, 2017). The chapter asserts that language has the potential to drive societal change, shaping cognitive fragments and social dynamics within specific space-time situations, leaving a lasting imprint on contemporary society. The issue of GBVAW serves as a tangible example, and the language used to frame it becomes a crucial focal point examined in chapters three and four of this book, which analyze international, regional, and national documents.

Therefore, it is essential to articulate an appropriate expression for Violence Perpetrated Against and Towards Women, one that acknowledges the prevailing gender imbalance and power dynamics. By emphasizing this characteristic, even in the formulation of the issue itself, and by examining how international organizations and governments have addressed GBVAW in their documents, laws, and policies until recently, it becomes possible to address its underlying causes. The role of international organizations and governments in presenting a specific social issue is of paramount importance, as it influences the responses and disparities in the development of GBVAW policies at the national level. This is exemplified by the case studies on GBVAW Government Responsiveness in Italy and Spain, which are presented in this book.

Chapter II

Methods of studying laws
and policies on GBVAW

Summary. Chapter II presents the research methodology that holds the research questions and research goal of the research and, hence, the book. It elucidates the reasons behind the multi-methods approach and explains all the methods that I used to carry out the research for this book.

This chapter is of fundamental importance since it explains the choices that have made possible: a) the analysis of the evolution of laws and policies on the phenomenon of GBVAW at the international level; b) the reason why the focus of the comparison is on GBVAW policies, and specifically the level of Government Responsiveness; c) and the reasons and modalities of the comparative analysis between two similar realities at the national level: Italy and Spain.

Introduction

This book applies a qualitative research methodology (Van Esch & Van Esch, 2013; Bhattacherjee, 2012) informed by an interpretative paradigm (Morse, 1997). A qualitative research methodology makes use of words more than numbers to foster the understandings of the reason behind one or multiple societal changes and events (Van Esch & Van Esch, 2013), in this case, the evolution of international, regional, and national documents on GBVAW, as well as the differences in policy-making in two selected countries: Spain and Italy. I chose to use and apply this research methodology because it enables to opt for adequate methodological procedures that allow for the study of the evolution and transformation in GBVAW laws and policies in different international (UN, CoE, EU) and national contexts (Italy and Spain) as well as over a specific time span (1993-2015). Furthermore, the fundamental tenet of the interpretive paradigm is the understanding that, unlike the subjects of research in the scientific sciences, social phenomena require understanding as well as just explanation (Smith, 1983). Hence, the interpretive paradigm was identified as the most research-appropriate due to its underlying potential to elicit new understandings of GBVAW within documents and policies as the expression of the societal changes around the concept and strategies to tackle it at both the international and national levels.

Finally, within the theoretical framework of the book, the choice of a qualitative research methodology allows the research questions postulated to be answered and the research goal to be satisfied in detail: to understand how international (UN) and regional (EU) documents on GBVAW, and the categories and expressions used within the documents (Eastel et al., 2012), contributed to different policies in countering GBVAW in Italy and Spain and, also, to highlight the reasons why the two countries responded differently (Government Responsiveness) to GBVAW.

Structure of the book

To answer the RQs, this book contains different phases that can be analytically described as follows.

The first phase is the description and qualitative text analysis of international documents that date from 1993, the year of the UN Vienna Declaration, also known as UN/GA Resolution 48/104 of 1993, to 2015, the year of the Sustainable Development Goals (SDGs), dealt with GBVAW. The next chapter of this book, chapter three, comprehensively focuses on the international debate on GBVAW that covers the documents of the United Nations (UN), the Council of Europe (CoE), and the European Union (EU). Through qualitative text analysis or qualitative content analysis, the chapter examines the main international and regional documents produced as part of International and European Law. It then looks at the policies and binding documents of the EU towards member states and internationally agreed resolutions with a special emphasis on the documents that have been welcomed in Italy and Spain, both binding and non-binding.

The book later discusses how both Spain and Italy translated and adopted the international documents on GBVAW in their national settings (Htun & Weldon, 2012; Roggeband, 2012; Montoya, 2013; Feci & Schettini, 2017), the influence of the latter in the creation of socially progressive policies in the single states (Valiente, 2005; Cimagalli, 2014; García, 2016; Corradi & Bandelli, 2018), and the innovations, additions or reductions of the documents in the national laws, policies and civil society's debates (Montoya, 2013; Walby et al., 2017). Furthermore, this last part of the book compares the two case studies, Spain and Italy, with reference to the degree of their Government Responsiveness and tries to capture the reasons for their diverse responses to the phenomenon of GBVAW in terms of laws and policies, accounting for the different international, national bodies and actors involved in the discussion of policies and legislative measures on GBVAW.

The choice behind these two case studies reflects the purpose of comparing similar cases (Dogan, 2002). Spain and Italy are two nation-states that belong to the Southern European model (Ferrera, 1996, 2005; Barbieri et al., 2015), defined by a so-called "traditional model" in which men work and provide the family's primary source of income while women provide a secondary source of income and take care of the household duties (Artazcoz et al., 2013). Moreover, Spain and Italy rank 25th and 29th, respectively, in the group of 62 nations with "extremely high human development" in the Gender Development Index and the Gender Inequality Index (UNDP 2019). In contrast, Spain and Italy are ranked 6th and 14th, respectively, on the EIGE Gender Equality Index (EIGE, 2021). They are often considered similar because of the social and public policies they choose to adopt (Esping-Andersen, 1990; Montoya, 2013; Cimagalli, 2014). However, the two countries present many dissimilarities in terms of Government Responsiveness and the capacity to tackle GBVAW. As in Htun and Weldon's study on VAW policies (2012), Italy's VAW responsiveness index has consistently ranked 0 (except for 2005, when it was rated 3), whereas Spain was rated 0 in 1975 before rising from 1 to 5 during the following decades (Annex A). The last chapter of this book has the intention to first describe and analyze the situation inside the territories of the two nation-states and, later, to compare the experiences and reactions to address GBVAW in Italy and Spain from 1993 to 2015.

The conclusions highlight the importance of the dialogue between multiple levels to tackle GBVAW from the UN to single states: Italy and Spain.

Methods

Multimethod research was chosen as a suitable approach for the book since it employs a combination of diverse methods or styles of research as opposed to limiting the book to the use of only one method (Brewer & Hunter, 1989, 2006; Anguera et al., 2018). Unlike mixed-method research, it is not limited to confining qualitative and quantitative methods but considers plenty of possibilities in the methodological combinations (Cameron Hay, 2016; Hunter & Brewer, 2015). To answer multiple research questions that were pertinent to a single piece of research, I set up multimethod qualitative research (Morse, 2003; Anguera et al., 2018) for this book, favoring solely qualitative methods (Bergman, 2007; Hesse-Biber et al., 2015). As multimethod research, I used a combination of qualitative methods (Collier & Elman, 2008; Seawright, 2016). For this book, the different methods are as listed as follows:

a) A careful identification and qualitative text analysis of international, regional, and national documents on GBVAW (laws, policies, documents, and conventions on the issue).

b) A reconstruction (process tracing as in Collier, 2011) and analysis of GBVAW policies with reference to the first aspect in policymaking (Government Responsiveness)

c)   A comparative analysis between GBVAW laws and policies in Italy and Spain in the period analyzed using process tracing.

d)   A series of in-depth interviews with targeted individuals who were involved in policies on GBVAW, namely: a) activists in movements and organizations; b) NGOs leaders and members; c) members of national and international institutions that work on GBVAW; d) researchers that work on GBVAW.

Ultimately, a multimethod research approach allows for the weaknesses and limitations of qualitative content analysis to be complemented by the strengths of GBVAW policies and Government Responsiveness description and analysis and, finally, in-depth interviews through the distilling, elaboration, and clarification of emergent categories and, eventually, comparison of case-studies.

Qualitative text analysis of documents

The description and analysis of the documents is the first phase of the book. During the first year of the research, I collected documents using keywords and literature from both international (UN, CoE) and regional documents (EU). Documents were retrieved from international, regional, and national platforms by first using single keywords and, later, by looking for co-occurrences.

The websites used for the study were:

-   The United Nations website (https://documents.un.org/prod/ods.nsf/home.xsp) for the United Nations.

-   The Council of Europe website (https://www.coe.int/en/web/cm/documents) for the texts approved by the Council of Europe.

-   The European Union website (https://europa.eu/european-union/documents-publications) was used to collect relevant documents and publications of the European Union.

Whereas during the second year of the research, I focused on the retrieval of national laws and policies on GBVAW. Italian national laws were collected from the Instituto Nazionale di Statistica website (https://www.istat.it/it/violenza-sulle-donne/il-contesto/normativa-italiana).

I retrieved Spanish national laws from the Ministerio the Igualdad website (https://violenciagenero.igualdad.gob.es/). Policies and national plans were found on the ministerial sites of the two countries and within a careful reconstruction of the evolutions of laws and policies (Collier, 2011; Roggeband, 2012) based on national parliamentary discussions and by reading the literature for the Italian and Spanish cases. Documents were selected according to the significance they had in the literature on GBVAW, in the media, in the normative, and by double checking the words presented in the documents with the use of keywords.

While starting the qualitative analysis of the texts, I paid attention to the semantic drift, change of perspective, and flexibility in considering the issue theoretically speaking and in the way it is addressed by international and regional organizations. Based on the literature review and considering the approaches familiar to Sociology and International Relations, these aspects are pivotal to pinpointing the phenomenon, recognizing the reasons behind systemic violence, and generating tools, policies, and strategies to fight GBVAW.

Subsequently, I selected sixteen documents for the UN, three for the CoE, and twenty-one for the EU. I started to work with codes and categories using as a tool the software Qualitative Data Analysis & Research Software ATLAS.ti[1] to qualitatively analyze my data for the first phase of the research. This tool allows to gather and analyze all the documents selected in the same hermeneutic unit and, therefore, improves the understanding of the evolution of the documents on the phenomenon in a broad way by creating links between the various documents taken into consideration through the use of codes and categories – supported by the theory and based on identifying important segments and assigning code labels in the documents (Smit, 2002; Friese, 2019) – thus considering both any manifest and latent contents in the documents (Wolff, 2004; Losito, 2007; Coffey, 2014), by understanding the complex meanings they might contain (Friese, 2019).

To study GBVAW in the international debate as well as identify the main differences between Italy and Spain, I selected the most relevant documents and proceeded with a first reading, paying attention to the theoretical framework coming from the literature and trying to recognize some elements that might have been overlooked from my studies and emerged from reading the texts. Then, I coded the different sections of the texts (Saldana, 2015), differentiating between codes, family codes, or coding frames and categories where categories are 'basic concepts of cognition' (Kuckartz, 2019, p. 184) and they subsume certain aspects that are common to the elements examined. Some of the categories were decided before the analysis in ATLAS.ti and refer to the so-called deductive or concept-driven categories.

The concept-driven categories in this book are Gender Violence; Violence Against Women; Violence towards Women; Male Violence against Women;

---

[1] Available at: http://www.atlasti.com/de.

Gender-Based Violence Against Women; Gender equality; Gender equity; Agency, and Empowerment.

I also decided to use 'in vivo codes' for the inductive (data-driven) part of the research to be represented in this phase of the investigation as they emerged in the single documents analyzed and as presented in chapters three and four of this book.

As for the quantitative content analysis, also in the qualitative analysis of the texts, the categories have two main roles. They serve as research tools and aid in the advancement of the study's theoretical framework (Lacity & Janson, 1994; Kuckartz, 2019, 2014). There are several types of categories, ranging from factual, thematic, evaluative, analytical, theoretical, and natural to formal ones. They present diverse characteristics. For example, as in Kuckartz (2014, pp. 31-39), factual categories represent actual situations or characteristics; thematic categories describe specific sections of the texts by giving labels to specific topics; evaluative categories often express ordinal scales of evaluation with reference to certain criteria; analytical categories go further than description and – intensively – scrutinize the materials in order to reach analytical categories; theoretical categories are a subgroup of analytical categories and relate to a specific existing theory; natural categories naturally arise from the 'field' as part of the 'in vivo codes' system; formal categories focus on the formal aspects of an analysis piece. This distinction has been considered to create categories when analyzing the text. These are the analytical categories for the book: Elimination of All Forms of Discrimination against Women, Women as a vulnerable group, Women's Empowerment, Preventive strategies, post-violence strategies, Male integration in the debate, and strategies to tackle GBVAW.

For this book, and specifically for the analysis of the texts, I first selected the material. Then, having in mind the research questions of the book, I carefully read the documents, started to create the coding frame, then coded the documents and analyzed them following a qualitative content analysis. These phases were constantly updated and revised on a circular basis, and in the third chapter of this study, I comprehensively present the results with reference to the international documents, followed by the case studies of Italy and Spain in the fourth chapter.

Field research

The field research was conducted in Spain and in Italy. It posed an emphasis on GBVAW policies identification and analysis – in terms of Government Responsiveness – to fight and prevent GBVAW (Htun & Weldon, 2012; Roggeband, 2012; Cimagalli, 2014) and on the comparison between the two countries from 1993 to 2015. It consisted of these phases:

a) Checking sites of government institutions and those of gender equality departments to have an overview of the main categories of reference and definitions of the phenomenon within the national contexts of Italy and Spain.

b) Identifying and analyzing the main national GBVAW law and policies (1993-2015).

c) Conducting in-depth, semi-structured interviews to targeted individuals, following the interview outline as in *Appendices 1*(in Italian) and *2* (in Spanish).

In the following subsections, I present the single phases of the research in greater detail.

General overview of governments institutions and gender equality departments sites

The first activity carried out in order to describe and analyze the evolution of laws and policies in the contexts of the two countries was a thorough search of the ministerial and governmental websites and gender equality departments of Spain and Italy. For Spain, the main point of reference is the site of the Ministerio de Igualdad (https://violenciagenero.igualdad.gob.es/), while for Italy, it is the site of the Instituto Nazionale di Statistica (https://www.istat.it/it/violenza-sulle-donne), but also the site of the Department for Equal Opportunities (http://www.pariopportunita.gov.it/). This first observation allowed us to understand the main categories of reference used by the two countries in reference to GBVAW from 1993 to 2015 and to observe the changes within the laws and policies of the two countries with greater clarity. In this first phase, I was able to understand some of the similarities and many of the differences that characterize these two countries, among them the total absence of subjects to whom the normative applies in many Italian laws, for instance, women. On the contrary, this lack of reference to subjects does not occur in Spain. In addition, the concept of gender, much used in Spain even in the early 2000s, is less evoked in Italian policies, if not before 2013.

GBVAW policies, Process tracing and Government Responsiveness

The book broadly considers the evolution of GBVAW laws and policies in the two countries (1993-2015) by describing and analyzing the main laws and policies on the issue, using tools of process tracing: careful reconstruction and description of the evolution of GBVAW national laws and policies (Collier, 2011; Roggeband, 2012), to later pinpoint the theoretical and analytical categories of references for the evolution of documents on GBVAW within the international community. Finally, by means of a comparative analysis between similar cases

(Dogan, 2002; Ferrera, 1996, 2005; Barbieri et al., 2015), any similarities and differences between the two countries were discussed. The book focuses on the first step in policymaking and, therefore, considers the level of Government Responsiveness since it represents the ability of governments to address the issue of Gender Violence Against Women by also responding to the demands of the international community. GR is the first step in policymaking. It is an expression of the interests – or the lack of it – that single nation-state governments put in place when GBVAW is at stake. As already mentioned in the theoretical framework, there is a way government responsiveness has been evaluated by scholars over recent years, especially thanks to the studies of Htun and Weldon (2012, 2013), who have extensively worked on an index of government responsiveness to VAW at the international level and the studies of Myrna Dawson at the Centre for the study of social and legal responses to violence[2] with an emphasis on Canada. I chose to compare the evolution of GBVAW laws and policies and refer to the index of GR since it helps towards a comparative overview of the differences and similarities between Italy and Spain.

In-depth interviews to targeted individuals

Finally, this book made use of in-depth, semi-structured interviews. In detail, after a careful study of the most suitable form of interview for this book – based on a consistent literature review (Corbetta, 1999; Blee & Taylor, 2002; Leavy, 2014) – the interviews carried out by the researcher were semi-structured, in-depth interviews (Kvale, 2007; Bichi, 2007). This type of interview asks all the respondents the same set of questions as in the outline of the interview (*Appendixes 1, 2*), but at the same time, respects the progression of the interview based on the experiences respondents chose to share with the interviewer. Furthermore, in-depth, semi-structured interviews allow not only to study the role of the words used by the respondents but also to read the evolution of the phenomenon analyzed, without standardizing what respondents share and, consequentially, by giving new perspectives on the issue (Bichi, 2000, 2007; King et al., 2018). Interviews are social activities that take place between a researcher and an individual, with the aim of disclosing some information on a specific issue and discovering pieces of socio-cultural realities (Corbetta, 1999; Bichi, 2007).

The interviews started in February 2020 in Spain during my research visiting period in Zaragoza, the capital of northeastern Spain's Aragon region. I carried out a total of 20 interviews, 10 in Spain and 10 in Italy. Due to the outbreak of

---

[2] For more information see: https://www.violenceresearch.ca/who/examining-regional-variations-social-and-legal-responsiveness-violence-against-women-canada

the COVID-19 pandemic in March 2020, part of the interviews took place in person, but the others were held online (Woodyatt et al., 2016; Nind et al., 2021). The interview outline was based on the same set of categories and codes as for the qualitative text analysis, which made up the previous phases of the book. The interviews were then transcribed verbatim and analyzed following the pattern of codes and categories identified in the previous phases of the book. The analytical, theoretical categories and thematic lines that emerged from the interviews were presented both in the discussion of the results as well as in the comparison between Italy and Spain, as described in chapter four.

In conclusion, in this pivotal chapter, I have presented the comprehensive research methodology that underlies the research questions and goals of this book. By elucidating the rationale behind adopting a multi-methods approach, I have provided a thorough explanation of the various methodologies employed to conduct the research.

This chapter holds immense significance as it lays the foundation for the following achievements:

a) Facilitating an in-depth analysis of the evolution of laws and policies pertaining to the phenomenon of GBVAW (Gender-Based Violence Against Women) on the international stage.

b) Establishing the justification for focusing on GBVAW policies, specifically in terms of Government Responsiveness, as a crucial element of comparison.

c) Unveiling the motives and intricacies underlying the comparative analysis between two closely aligned national realities, namely Italy and Spain.

By delving into the intricacies of the research methodology, this chapter serves as a vital bridge, enabling the exploration and understanding of the aforementioned accomplishments.

Chapter III

The international debate on GBVAW

Summary: This chapter on the evolution of international, inter-regional, and regional documents on GBVAW reveals the different ways in which the phenomenon has been addressed by the various organizations: from a purely private issue to a problem that undermines equality between men and women up to the gender mainstreaming approach. The latter considers the gender variable within policies and does not consider women merely as vulnerable subjects and victims but also as subjects with an agency. Regarding the relations among states, the evolving approach among the various bodies moves from the consideration of GBVAW as a problem to be dealt with at the national level, especially in the UN documents of the first years, to a greater emphasis, clear at a CoE level, and recently resumed – especially with the Daphne programs by the European Union – towards the sharing of best policy practices and an interconnected effort among MSs.

Introduction

This chapter aims to discuss the evolution of the documents adopted by the international community to fight Gender-Based Violence Against Women (GBVAW).

The starting points of this chapter are the United Nations (UN) declarations, conventions, and resolutions. In detail, the first paragraph of this section starts with the 48/104 UN Resolution of 1993 declared by the General Assembly and ends with the SDGs in 2015, especially with reference to SDG 16 and SDG 5, which contain specific goals to contrast GBVAW.

The chapter continues to analyze the most relevant documents of the Council of Europe (CoE) on the issues related to the fight and prevention of GBVAW, as well as the different bodies of the European Union (EU), which – throughout the decades – were able to influence the progress of societies by producing cultural, societal and political transformation on the matter (Montoya, 2013; Feci & Schettini, 2017). To conclude, by means of a theoretical investigation of GBVAW and qualitative content analysis of the documents, this chapter tries to show how the international community dealt with GBVAW from 1993 to 2015 and, in the following chapter, the influence the UN, CoE, and EU had on Italy and Spain, by adopting a top-down perspective: from the international to the regional level.

This chapter considers 16 documents of the United Nations, the most important three documents of the inter-regional organization of the Council of Europe, and 21 texts of the European Union (EU Parliament, Council of the EU, EU Commission). Table 3.1 presents the documents and their specificity referred to the UN. Table 3.2 provides an overview of the conventions and resolutions of the Council of Europe, and Table 3.3 makes specific reference to the evolution of the documents as produced by the different bodies of the EU.

This chapter discusses the content of these resolutions and documents of the UN, CoE, and EU by using the Qualitative Data Analysis & Research Software ATLAS.ti.[1] This software allows for the implementation of qualitative content analysis, thanks to the creation of some practical codes (in-vivo codes) or inductive categories, significant in starting to analyze the way the phenomenon was intended and addressed by the different organizations in the period analyzed, and later to add descriptive and analytical categories that are discussed throughout the chapter and the whole book.

The concept-driven categories (or deductive categories) in this chapter and book are: Gender Violence; Violence Against Women; Violence towards Women; Male Violence against Women; Gender-Based Violence Against Women; Gender equality; Gender equity; Agency, and Empowerment.

The analytical categories that combine both the deductive and inductive ones and are more specific to the book's scope and aims are: Elimination of All Forms of Discrimination against Women, Women as a vulnerable group, Women's empowerment, Preventive strategies, Post-violence strategies, Male integration in the debate and strategies to tackle GBVAW.

The categories represent a set of tools that serve to display the main thematic lines of interest that the international community adopted to contrast the phenomenon from 1993 to 2015, especially those theoretical references that are both directly and implicitly mentioned in the documents, political strategies (from international to regional) to curb GBVAW and, policies to contrast (fight and prevent) the phenomenon of GBVAW. This book reexamines the same categories and thematic lines in the specific chapter on the cases of Italy and Spain, chapter four, and tries to understand the influence the documents adopted by the international community had on the Italian and Spanish laws and policies on GBVAW, in terms of specific measures and policies adopted, and categories used (as in the language choices, theoretical references and thematic lines).

---

[1] Available at: http://www.atlasti.com/de

UN documents

The United Nations is an international body of global importance that, especially after the end of World War II, and therefore replacing the League of Nations created immediately after the First World War, aims to maintain relations between countries as peacefully as possible. It consists of six main bodies: the General Assembly (UN deliberative, policy-making, and representative organ), the Security Council (UN operative organ), the Economic and Social Council (ECOSOC), the Trusteeship Council, the International Court of Justice, and the UN Secretariat. The UN also has several sub-organs that play distinct roles but aspire to the same objectives of international cooperation, harmonization of the actions of nations, and global peace and security. The United Nations (UN) plays a crucial role in addressing gender-based violence (GBV) by promoting international standards, advocating for policy changes, providing support to survivors, and coordinating efforts among member states and stakeholders. There are some key aspects of the UN's role in addressing GBVAW. For instance, the UN has developed a robust normative framework to address GBVAW. This includes the Universal Declaration of Human Rights, the 1979 Convention on the Elimination of All Forms of Discrimination Against Women (CEDAW), and the Declaration on the Elimination of Violence against Women. CEDAW defines discrimination against women as any distinction, exclusion, or restriction based on sex that impairs or nullifies the enjoyment of human rights and fundamental freedoms. The convention emphasizes the need for gender equality, challenging societal norms, stereotypes, and harmful practices that perpetuate gender-based discrimination. Furthermore, CEDAW establishes a monitoring mechanism through the Committee on the Elimination of Discrimination Against Women. State parties are required to submit regular reports to the committee detailing the progress made in implementing the provisions of the convention. The committee provides guidance, recommendations, and expertise to countries, fostering accountability and supporting efforts to address gender inequality. These instruments provide a foundation for recognizing and addressing GBVAW as a human rights violation. The UN also works to raise awareness about GBVAW and advocates for policies and laws that protect and empower women and girls. It supports member states in developing national action plans, legislation, and strategies to prevent and respond to GBVAW effectively. Furthermore, the UN encourages the collection of reliable and disaggregated data on GBVAW to inform evidence-based policies and programs. It supports research initiatives and strengthens data systems to improve understanding of the prevalence, causes, and consequences of GBVAW. It provides technical assistance, capacity building, and resources to member states to strengthen their institutional response to GBVAW. This support includes training for law enforcement officials, judiciary, health workers, and other professionals. More importantly, the UN acts as a platform for coordination and collaboration among member states, UN agencies, civil society organizations, and other stakeholders working on the issue. It facilitates dialogue, knowledge sharing, and joint initiatives to address GBVAW comprehensively. Finally, the UN leads global campaigns, such as the "Orange the World" campaign during the 16 Days of Activism against Gender-Based Violence, to raise awareness about GBV, challenge harmful norms and stereotypes, and mobilize action to end violence against women and girls. In addition, the UN's 2030 Agenda for Sustainable Development includes the SDGs, which explicitly recognize the importance of gender equality and the elimination of violence against women and girls as key goals. The UN works with member states to integrate GBV prevention and response into national development plans and initiatives. Through these various efforts, the UN seeks to promote gender equality, prevent GBV, ensure survivors' access to justice and support services, and create a world free from all forms of violence and discrimination against women and girls. Regarding the specific issue analyzed in this book – GBVAW – the chapter describes and analyzes 16 documents produced by different organs of the UN, starting with the first clear Resolution of 1993 that contains a definition of violence perpetrated against women, and ending with the SDGs in 2015, which also contain some important targets countering VAW/GV/GBVAW.

The table below shows the main documents selected for the analysis of the evolution of UN documents on VAW/GV/GBVAW from 1993 to 2015.

Table 3.1 UN: documents on VAW/GV/GBVAW (1993-2015)[2]

UN: DOCUMENTS ON GBVAW (1993-2015)				
YEAR	BODY	SYMBOL	TITLE	TYPOLOGY
1993	UN/GA	A/RES/48/104	Declaration on the Elimination of VAW	Resolution
1995	UN/GA	A/CONF.177/20/Rev.1	Beijing Declaration-Fourth World Conference in Women	Declaration and Platform for action
1999	UN/GA	A/RES/52/87--- 54/134 2000	International Day for the Elimination of Violence against Women	Resolution
2000	UN/GA	A/RES/55/68	Elimination of all forms of violence, including crimes against women	Resolution

---

[2] Tab. 3.1. shows the most relevant UN documents dealing wih GBVAW from 1993 to 2015. The table is the author's own output.

2000	UN/GA	A/RES/55/66	Working towards the elimination of crimes against women committed in the name of honour	Resolution
2002	UN/ESC	E/CN.4/Sub.2/2002/43	Report submitted by the UN Population Fund- Economic, social and cultural rights prevention of discrimination	Report
2005	UN/ESC	E/CN.6/2006/10; E/CN.4/2006/60	Report of the UN Development Fund for Women on the elimination of VAW	Report
2005	UN/GA	A/RES/60/140/GA- Final Report	Beijing +10- Final report - Follow-up to the 4th World Conference on Women	Report
2006	UN/GA	A/RES/61/143	Intensification of efforts to eliminate all forms of VAW	Resolution
2007	UN/GA	A/RES/62/133	Eliminating rape and other forms of sexual violence in all their manifestations, including in conflict and related situations	Resolution
2009	UN/GA	A/RES/64/137	Intensification of efforts to eliminate all forms of VAW	Resolution
2010	UN/HRC	A/HRC/RES/15/23	Elimination of discrimination against women	Resolution
2013	UN/GA	A/RES/68/191	Taking action against gender-related killing of women and girls	Resolution
2015	UN/HRC	A/HRC/29/3	Report of the UNE for Gender Equality and VAW	Report
2015	UN/HRC	A/HRC/32/3	Report of the UNE for Gender Equality and VAW	Report
2015	UN/GA	A/RES/70/1	Transforming our world: the 2030 Agenda for Sustainable Development	Resolution

Analysis of selected documents

a)   **1993, Resolution "Declaration on the Elimination of VAW" (48/104 UN/GA)**

This Resolution is of pivotal importance for many reasons. In Article 1 of this UN document, also known as the Declaration on the Elimination of Violence Against Women (DEVAW) or Vienna Declaration, there is the first internationally agreed definition of Violence perpetrated Against Women. Article one declares that:

> The term "violence against women" means any act of gender-based violence that results in, or is likely to result in, physical, sexual, or psychological harm or suffering to women, including threats of such acts, coercion, or arbitrary deprivation of liberty, whether occurring in public or in private life.

This conceptualization of the phenomenon is still the main point of reference when addressing the issue of violence in relation to women at the international, regional, and national levels – as in the case of Italian laws and policies. The Resolution gives a sort of taxonomy, division in forms and categories, to easily identify VAW and a series of instruments to fight it. The stress given by the Resolution mostly refers to the national level of action, which results significant, with it also being considered the most relevant. DEVAW also questions the lack of policies and laws regulating the phenomenon of VAW and, therefore, envisages a Plan of Rehabilitation for both perpetrators and victims. However, the possibilities of carrying out these actions result unclear. Throughout the whole document, the word elimination is more frequent than prevention, as a demonstration that tools to act at a cultural, preventive level are not yet considered as the focus. This aspect of the Resolution and the focus it established has mapped out the structure of following debates on women's issues and GBVAW as with the Millennium Development Goals (MDGs) and, later, with the Sustainable Development Goals (SDGs). From the early 1990s, and especially for the UN, equality, as part of women's rights to end all forms of discrimination, has been a crucial element of the preferred theoretical approach used to address violence at the international level, namely VAW. Moreover, this first resolution, by moving towards the elimination of all forms of discrimination against women, relates new aspects to the world of equality: security, liberty, integrity, and dignity of all human beings.

b)   **1995, "Beijing Declaration and Platform for Action "Fourth World Conference on Women" (A/CONF.177/20/Rev.1 UN/GA)**

The 1995 Beijing Declaration on Women presents a specific Plan of Action for women's empowerment in global societies. It also includes a specific subsection on violence perpetrated towards women. Section D of the Declaration deals with definitions, state of the art, tactics, and strategies as useful tools to address VAW/GV/GBVAW. The final document of the conference in Beijing shows interesting reflection opportunities for the discussion on the issues related to and directly referred to mostly VAW. For example, in the first paragraph, it asserts that the existence of VAW constitutes an obstacle to the goal of equality, development, and peace. It also adds: "it violates and impairs or nullifies the enjoyment by women of their human rights and fundamental freedoms." The second paragraph of the specific section on VAW of the Plan defines VAW in these terms:

> Any act of gender-based violence that results in, or is likely to result in, physical, sexual or psychological harm or suffering to women, including threats of such acts, coercion, or arbitrary deprivation of liberty, whether occurring in public or private life.

In the discussion presented in this document, it is revealed how "Violence against women is a manifestation of the historically unequal power relations between men and women" (A/RES/48/104, Declaration on the Elimination of Violence against Women, 1993). It is evident how, since the 1990s, the link between power relations, gender gap closure, and VAW/GV/GBVAW has been taken for granted. The document also considers measures to prevent and eliminate VAW that move from active promotion of strategies to eliminating and preventing GBVAW to means of support for violated women, legislations, calls for actions upon states, as well as the involvement of the whole international community, also concerning the improvement of data collection on VAW in order to create policies against acts of violence.

c) 1999, Resolution "International Day for the Elimination of Violence against Women" (A/RES/52/87--- 54/134 2000 UN/GA)

In 1999, the General Assembly institutionalized the "International Day for the Elimination of Violence against Women." For instance, the text asserts the concern of the states in seeing (GB)VAW as an "obstacle" towards equality and highlights the rooted historical unbalanced power situation in contemporary society as a cause of violence and societal-based constructions, triggering acts of (GB)VAW. A reference that is more in line with the paradigm of GV (Taylor & Jasinski, 2011) compared to the more flexible one of VAW (Casique & Furegato, 2006), despite the expression used to denote the issue being the latter. Moreover, at the UN level, a crucial tool acting as a transnational action-based strategy against GBVAW considered in the aforementioned set of Resolutions was the 1999 Optional Protocol to the 1979 Convention on the Elimination of All Forms of Discrimination against Women (CEDAW). It allowed single individuals to make a complaint to the international community in the name of the UN when either the national options are over, or the nation-state of reference is not addressing the complaint. CEDAW has the key role in making a judgment on the objection and tackling the issue in case human rights violations are in place (Weldon, 2006).

d)   2000, Resolution "Elimination of all forms of violence, including crimes against women" (A/RES/55/68 UN/GA)

Resolution 55/68 of the same year, on the elimination of all forms of violence against women and girls, focuses on the existence of a relationship based on a positive correlation between Women's empowerment and the elimination of GBVAW. It also expresses an appreciation for the work, the campaigns, and the efforts of different sections of society, from women's organizations and movements to community-based organizations and individuals, in making an effort to prevent and combat VAW in all its forms, accounting for more than just physical violence and reaching out to economic and psychological ones. Moreover, in this document, the preference in the use of the "word-concept" of women and of VAW is visible. All forms of violence are accounted for, and the UN/GA asserts to "devote attention" to this issue towards women, both in public and private life, as in the debate of nation-states and their reports to the Committee on the Elimination of Discrimination against Women.

e)   2000, Resolution "Working towards the elimination of crimes against women committed in the name of honor" (A/RES/55/66 UN/GA)

Resolution 55/66 of 2000 of the United Nations General Assembly, called "Working towards the elimination of crimes against women committed in the name of honor," is thought-provoking since it has a clear nation-state level of analysis and a direct call for action upon MSs. At the same time, the fascinating point in the document is the idea of a comprehensive dialogue between local non-governmental organizations, civil society, and the international community. Operative clauses inside the Resolution "call upon" the totality of UN nation-states to act towards the implementation of human rights-based obligations, to consider support services and institutional mechanisms for those women who have been victims or have been threatened of crimes against them, committed in the name of honor. Women are the main subject of the resolution. Crimes considered in its formulation strictly relate to the will of preventing and wiping out crimes perpetrated in the name of honor. Cultural underpinnings are a visible part of the theoretical approach used in the Resolution, which swings between VAW and Gender Violence.

f)   2002, Report "Economic, social and cultural rights prevention of discrimination" (E/CN.4/Sub.2/2002/43 UN/ESC)

The report "Economic, social and cultural rights prevention of discrimination" is of crucial significance due to the call of the document to use the Trust Fund in Support of Actions to Eliminate Violence Against Women, created in 1996, to supplement laws and decrees in the legislative field with the trainings and reforms of criminal justice systems. The focus of the report is addressing "ways to incorporate approaches to gender-based violence into reproductive healthcare planning." Gender perspective and mainstreaming appear of vital importance in the text of the Commission on Human Rights, in the sense that the aim is "to integrate gender into policy formulation" (Walby et al., 2017). The European Union, in its strategy to tackle VAW, will also use this specific point of policy creation by national and regional bodies, for instance, the EIGE (Montoya, 2013; Feci & Schettini, 2017). The enjoyment of human rights and violence are considered as negatively correlated to each other. The terminology preferred in this report is Gender-based violence, and the sub-terminology mostly accounted for is the one of physical violence within the broader topics of the trafficking and health care of women.

g)   2005, Report "on the elimination of violence against women" (E/CN.4/2006/60, E/CN.6/2006/10 UN/ESC)

The report "on the elimination of violence against women" addresses the development and evolution made in the sector of eliminating VAW by referring to the UN/GA mandate given with Resolution 50/166 of 1995 to the UNIFEM (United Nations Development Fund for Women). There are two main directions of the fund to connect strategies, create good practices and lessons, and open the space for replication and widespread opportunities. The document calls for "a public awareness campaign and the training of volunteers to provide legal aid and counselling" (p. 4) to implement the renewed domestic violence law and respect the enjoyment of human rights for all sections of society. It gives decisive interest in the enhancement and implementation of laws and policies at regional and sub-regional levels, considering gender equality pivotal in tackling the spreading of the phenomenon (York, 2011). It concludes that VAW "is the most pervasive violation of human rights" (p. 7) and that "the progress for women is essential to achieving all internationally agreed development goals" (p. 8). Thus, the UN and the Fund emphasize the will to continue supporting governments and regional apparatus in implementing laws, policies, and good practices to dismantle the rhetoric and perpetration of acts of violence against one part of society, namely women.

h)   2005, Report "Follow-up to the 4th World Conference on Women" (A/RES/60/140/GA UN/GA)

The Resolution focuses on gender equality strategies and approaches, as well as Women's empowerment, by calling upon the interconnected cooperation of nation-states, the United Nations, and other organizations. Despite the reference to other levels of organization appearing in the text, the national level of emphasis is more decisive in addressing the promotion of Women's empowerment and pursuing Gender Equality. By adopting a gender mainstreaming approach and reaching out to "the full realization of all human rights... the full representation and full and equal participation of women in political, social and economic decision-making in society" (Preambulatory clauses, p. 2), the UN integrates a strategy to address the main issue of women's advancement in contemporary societies with the commitment of both men and women. Socio-economic policies and welfare dynamics at national and regional levels, as in the appointment of policies in pursuing gender equality and implementing the platform of action created during Beijing 1995, are envisaged as tools to prevent GBVAW. The mutual participation of institutional, governmental, and non-governmental bodies of the society in the different contexts of the world is considered a key element towards the prevention and, hence, eradication of GBVAW as well as the enhancement of women's rights.

i)   2006, Resolution "Intensification of efforts to eliminate all forms of VAW" (A/RES/61/143 UN/GA)

The Resolution "Intensification of efforts to eliminate all forms of VAW" invokes the protection of human rights and the full enjoyment of fundamental freedoms, as well as the condemnation of all forms of discrimination based on sex, as in the Charter of the United Nations, and reflects on VAW as "rooted in historically unequal power relations" which goes accordingly to the paradigm of Gender Violence focusing on one layer of causality. Custom, traditions, or religious considerations are not excuses for the perpetration of acts of violence, as declared in the text, with the public and private actors being in no case exempted. Ending impunity, fostering leadership, and educating on gender equality by adopting a comprehensive and systematic approach inside national plans of policies are seen as pillar elements in the fight against violence. The General Assembly (GA) also requests the Secretary-General to put in place measures to monitor the phenomenon of violence towards women. Firstly, by using a cross-national database based on effectiveness, implementation, and impact to prevent and eliminate GBVAW. Secondly, by incorporating with assessable tools the "possible indicators" on GBVAW, welcoming the campaigns to address and tackle the issue. Finally, the Resolution also points out that the exclusion of women from social policies endangers vulnerability towards violence, thus recalling for greater gender equality.

j) **2007, Resolution "Eliminating rape and other forms of sexual violence in all their manifestations, including in conflict and related situations" (A/RES/62/133 UN/GA)**

The Resolution "Eliminating rape and other forms of sexual violence in all their manifestations, including in conflict and related situations" recalls the steps the international community, especially through campaigns, has taken to find social policies and share best practices in the fight against sexual violence.

The emphasis is on the cooperation between countries and shared best practices to hamper VAW/GV/GBVAW occurrences globally. The Resolution is of fundamental importance because it highlights how sexual violence is not a private matter but a public one and that the international community and individual states must act to prevent it from being used as a tool for imposing force and power, even in conflict and related situations.

k) **2009, Resolution "Intensification of efforts to eliminate all forms of VAW" (A/RES/64/137 UN/GA)**

Campaigns, more inclusive social policies, and the sharing of best practices are encouraged to eliminate all forms of VAW. There is specific attention on public strategies and international campaigns to be implemented as a first step to counter VAW compared to previous Resolutions, as well as the idea that more inclusive social policies will empower women and allow VAW rates to decrease. This shows a slight change in perspective on the most appropriate measures to combat VAW.

l) **2010, Resolution "Elimination of discrimination against women" (A/HRC/RES/15/23 UN/GA)**

The Resolution "Elimination of discrimination against women," adopted by the Human Rights Council in 2010, focuses on the elimination of discrimination against women and men-women inequality as a power relation (York, 2011). In detail, the Resolution declares that there still are "de jure and de facto discriminatory laws and practices" (Preambulatory clauses, p. 2). Equality is still far from being a reality. The states are considered the main actors in fostering policies and strategies to eliminate discrimination against women, and the UN is just "contributing" to their endeavors. The Resolution establishes a working group on the topic, made up of experts with a three-year duration, to "promote and exchange views on best practices" (p. 4) and foster cooperation among countries. It is interesting to notice in the document the prevalence of the word "against" in reference to women, with a strong terminological emphasis on what suggests a lack of women's agency. Resolution 15/40 of the

Human Rights Council declares that women are not required to have proofs of resistance against violent acts, assaults, or rape, thus representing a step forward in defining the different forms of violence and protecting women from GBVAW.

m) 2013, Resolution "Taking action against gender-related killing of women and girls" (A/RES/68/191 UN/GA)

This Resolution deals with physically violent acts which end in gender-related killings (also called feminicides or femicides) of women and girls. It claims that MSs do not punish those who commit such violence in their national legislation. The international community is "alarmed by the fact that violence against women and girls is among the least punished crimes in the world" (p. 3). Therefore, there is an urgent need for prevention and investigation with the precise aim of eliminating GBVAW in all its forms. The crucial role of criminal justice in fighting feminicides should also be integrated through studies, data collection, analysis, and tools for better practices, as provided by academia. There is a new interest in the work of the researchers to be active participants and actors of change in dealing with the measures to counter violence against women and girls.

n) 2015, Report "Report of the UNE for Gender Equality and VAW" (A/HRC/29/3 UN/HRC)

This report is of paramount importance since it sets priorities on how to improve women's conditions in the enjoyment of their full rights by understanding the causes behind GBVAW and promoting public and private responses to achieve gender equality and parity.

The report envisages national, regional, and cross-regional calls for action and a focus on analysis to understand the causes behind VAW/GV, therefore focusing on preventive more than just post-violence measures and strategies.

o) 2015, Report "Report of the UNE for Gender Equality and VAW" (A/HRC/32/3 UN/HRC)

The Report considers multisector strategies to be the most effective for the Member states within coordinated communication practices among civil society and governments, and where the Fund commits to bridging the gap between discourse and application. There is a call for awareness and joint efforts to address gender-based violence, which remains a human rights crisis, according to the report A/HRC/32/3. The Resolution makes specific reference to the achievement of the Sustainable Development Goals (SDGs). Community mobilization approaches are welcomed to reach a change in behaviors, attitudes and improve tools to tackle GBVAW, especially by preventing violent behaviors among young cohorts and by integrating both men and women in the debate: cultural changes are – thus – at the basis for countering GBVAW.

p) 2015, Resolution "Transforming our world: the 2030 Agenda for Sustainable Development" (A/RES/70/1)

Finally, SDGs have a focus on women's empowerment and the fight against VAW/GV/GBVAW. Specifically, within SDG 16, there is Target 16.1, which aims to: "Significantly reduce all forms of violence and related death rates everywhere" (p. 25), and Target 16.3 that focuses on the promotion of "the rule of law at the national and international levels and ensure equal access to justice for all" (p. 29). Moreover, SDG 5 (5.2) includes a target to eliminate all forms of violence against women and girls by 2030.

Categories and thematic lines within UN documents on VAW/GV/GBVAW

Following a chronological order of the UN documents on VAW/GV/GBVAW, there are interesting aspects to point out.

From 1993 to 2000, there was a clear definition of the phenomenon, and VAW was considered a human rights violation and an obstacle to gender equality. In the same period, there was the institution of the "International Day for the Elimination of VAW" and Resolutions, as well as conventions, that directly called for action to nation-states and dialogue between different entities. Both VAW and GV as theoretical approaches and concept-driven categories are visible. There is flexibility in the discussion on violence perpetrated against women with a strong reference to the main characteristics of GV, but VAW is quoted more often.

In the period that goes from 2001 to 2005, there was a stronger integration of gender perspective into policy formulation, and VAW is considered "the most pervasive violation of human rights." The emphasis is placed on the development of good practices, public awareness campaigns, training of volunteers, and legal aid, as well as counselling within a gender mainstreaming perspective.

From 2006 to 2010, there is a clear reference to the fact that the exclusion of women from social policies endangers vulnerability towards violence. Therefore, inequality in social relations and the persistence of discriminatory laws and practices are at the basis of violence perpetrated toward women. There is also a visible semantic drift in the documents that prefer Gender Violence instead of Violence Against Women.

Finally, in 2011-2015, the UN recognized that GBVAW is "among the least punished crimes in the world" and called for action from national, regional, and cross-regional entities. Multisector strategies are encouraged, with there being a more evident emphasis on preventive strategies in the discussion and on the possible ways to contrast GV/VAW/GBVAW, as well as the shift in perspective from women only as a vulnerable group to a greater emphasis on their empowerment and agency.

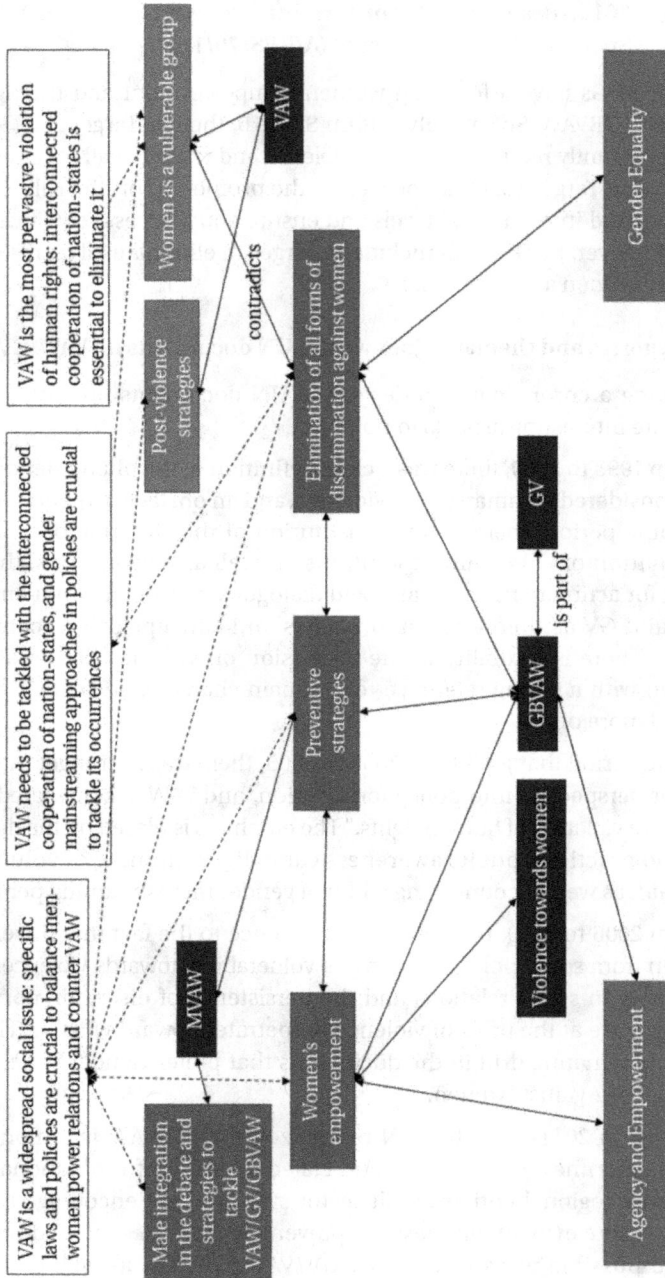

Fig. 3.1 UN Documents on VAW/GV/GBVAW: categories and thematic lines

Figure 3.1. shows the main concept-driven and analytical categories that emerged from the analysis as well as the interrelation among them and the thematic lines that give a snapshot of the main themes treated by the United Nations in the period analyzed. At the beginning of Figure 3.1, there are three prevailing thematic lines, in violet and pink the analytical categories (Viole⁻: women's empowerment and preventive as well as comprehensive policies on GBVAW), in blue, with different gradations, the main theoretical categories (Dark blue for definitions of the phenomenon and light blue for related categories).

These are the thematic lines that emerged from the analysis:

Definition and Categorization of Violence Against Women (VAW)

The selected documents highlight the importance of having a clear definition of VAW. The 1993 UN Resolution "Declaration on the Elimination of VAW" and the 1995 "Beijing Declaration and Platform for Action" provide internationally agreed definitions that encompass physical, sexual, and psychological harm or suffering to women. These definitions serve as a point of reference at the international, regional, and national levels. The documents also emphasize the need for categorization and Gender-Based Power Relations. In addition, a recurring theme across the documents is the recognition of violence against women as a manifestation of historically unequal power relations between men and women. The 1995 Beijing Declaration explicitly states that VAW violates women's human rights and fundamental freedoms, hindering their equality, development, and peace. This understanding of power relations shapes the approach to addressing VAW and highlights the importance of addressing gender inequality and promoting women's empowerment.

Prevention, Elimination, and Rehabilitation

The documents emphasize the need for both prevention and elimination of VAW. While the focus on elimination is more frequent than prevention, it is acknowledged that cultural and preventive measures are crucial. The documents also highlight the importance of rehabilitation for both perpetrators and victims of VAW, envisioning a comprehensive approach to addressing the issue.

International Cooperation and Multilevel Action

The resolutions call for international cooperation and coordination to address VAW effectively. They emphasize the involvement of nation-states, the international community, non-governmental organizations, and civil society in combating VAW. The documents stress the importance of regional and sub-regional policies and the sharing of best practices to eliminate VAW.

Gender Mainstreaming and Gender Equality

Gender mainstreaming is a key approach advocated in the documents, emphasizing the integration of gender perspectives into policy formulation and decision-making processes. The resolutions highlight the need for gender equality and the full participation of women in political, social, and economic spheres. The elimination of discrimination against women is a central goal, emphasizing the importance of addressing systemic gender-based inequalities.

Intersectionality and Comprehensive Approach

Some documents acknowledge the intersectionality of VAW, considering various aspects such as cultural, religious, and societal factors that contribute to violence. The resolutions call for comprehensive approaches that consider different forms of violence, including physical, sexual, economic, and psychological. The recognition of the interconnectedness of VAW with other human rights violations and development goals is emphasized. Identification of different forms of VAW, enabling easier recognition and addressing of the issue.

Human Rights-Based Approach

The resolutions consistently frame VAW as a violation of human rights and emphasize the importance of protecting and promoting the human rights of women. They call for the end of impunity, the monitoring of VAW, and the integration of human rights perspectives into policies and programs.

Overall, these resolutions have had a significant impact on shaping the global response to GBVAW. They have provided a common language, conceptual framework, and set of strategies for addressing VAW at the international, regional, and national levels. The thematic analysis reveals a progression from defining and categorizing GBVAW to emphasizing prevention, gender equality, international cooperation, and the protection of human rights. However, challenges remain in effectively implementing the strategies outlined in these resolutions and achieving the goal of eliminating GBVAW worldwide.

CoE documents

The Council of Europe is a continental (Europe), inter-regional human rights organization. It is not an EU organization, although it is often confused as such. It was founded on May 5, 1949, with the aim of promoting democracy, human rights, and the rule of law. It is part of the regional European Human Rights mechanism, and its purposes are the respect of human rights, democracy, and the rule of law in Europe. One of the most significant contributions of the Council of Europe is the European Convention on Human Rights (ECHR), adopted in 1950. The ECHR establishes a legal framework for the protection of human rights, and it is overseen by the European Court of Human Rights (ECtHR), which is an institution of the Council of Europe. Individuals who believe their rights have been violated can bring cases before the ECtHR after exhausting domestic legal remedies. The Council of Europe also works to combat various forms of discrimination and to counter GBVAW. As is often the case with public international law, the CoE does not have the power to make binding laws, but it does have the authority to enforce international agreements as decided among CoE Member States (currently 47 states).

The three documents, as in Table 3.2, constitute the pillar stones in the achievement of women's rights and in the fight against acts of discrimination and GBVAW as produced and signed by the CoE Member States.

Insert Table 3.2 approximately here

Table 3.2 Council of Europe: documents on VAW/GV/GBVAW[3]

COUNCIL OF EUROPE: DOCUMENTS ON VAW/GV/GBVAW		
YEAR	TITLE	TYPOLOGY
2002	Recommendation on the protection of Women against Violence Rec (2002)5	Recommendation
2005	Convention on Action against Trafficking in human beings	Convention
2011	Convention on preventing and combating violence against women and domestic violence (of Istanbul)	Convention

Analysis of selected documents: Council of Europe

a) 2002, Recommendation on "the protection of Women against Violence" Rec (2002)5

The 2002 Recommendation on "the protection of Women against Violence" of the Committee of Ministers to MSs emphasizes the protection of women against violence. In the preamble, the text uses the expression "violence towards women" and addresses the issue of "imbalance of power" existing at both societal and familiar levels between men and women (Baker & Leicht, 2017; York, 2011). The recommendation focuses on active educational training, public awareness campaigns, and men's role in ending violence. It also firmly encourages national policies against violence towards women and the creation of a body controlling "the implementation of measures to combat violence" as a cooperation approach, as well as the role of media and modern technologies in avoiding the promotion of the "stereotyped image of men and women."

---

[3] Tab. 3.2. shows the most relevant CoE documents dealing wih GBVAW from 1993 to 2015. The table is the author's own output.

However, the measures proposed seem utopist, especially with reference to the role of media. For instance, according to the recommendation, MSs should:

> Encourage the media to promote a non-stereotyped image of women and men based on respect for the human person and human dignity and to avoid programmes associating violence and sex; as far as possible, these criteria should also be taken into account in the field of the new information technologies. (p. 8)

As can be deduced from a closer reading of the text, the media have the role of imposing a non-stereotypical vision of men and women that, therefore, reduces, at a utopian level, the occurrences of Violence towards Women. However, the meaning of a non-stereotypical view of women and men is not specified – therefore avoiding that it depends on the specific societies and contexts of MSs (Feci & Schettini, 2017; González, 2012) – and there is also no space left for the individual to develop his/her own understanding of the phenomenon since, according to the recommendation and thanks to the role of media, the message against VAW/GBVAW is clear and comprehensive. There is a veiled censorship, which appears not very realistic, especially when considering a society where technology is overlapping and integrated into people's life, as is and was already in 2002, and violence is physical but mostly symbolic in the way it is conceptualized but also in the strategies envisages to counter the same (Bourdieu, 2001).

To some extent, the recommendation is innovative and comprehensive in terms of the way it describes violence. For example, it considers both women's agency and empowerment by preferring the expression "towards women" instead of "against": women are not only seen as victims of violence, but they can also change the situation of violence they experience. At the same time, the recommendation is a bit naïve in the way it wants and aims to address GBVAW (i.e., compensation, the role of media, using a genetic database of perpetrators).

b)   2005, Convention on "action against the trafficking in human beings."

The Convention on Action against Trafficking in Human Beings of 2005 focuses on both gender equality and gender mainstreaming approaches to end trafficking in human beings. In this respect, the Convention firmly condemns those practices that are directed at women and affect their integrity as human beings endowed with rights and freedoms. The Convention also aims to promote international cooperation to act against the trafficking of human beings, considering VAW/GV deriving from trafficking as one of the fundamental issues to be addressed.

c) **2011, Convention on "preventing and combating violence against women and domestic violence"**

The most notable document describing and addressing VAW/GV/GBVAW is the "Council of Europe Convention on preventing and combating violence against women and domestic violence," also known as the 2011 Istanbul Convention. Its main aim is the coordination among MSs to prevent and end acts of violence toward women in both public and private spaces. It is a legally binding measure to all the MSs of the CoE who signed the document. Article 3 presents the definition of both acts and actors related to violence perpetrated against different subjects. This legal tool specifically mentions the expression of VAW and gender-based violence (GV and GBVAW). The Convention moves across addressing the so-called "4 Ps approach": protection, prevention, and persecution, respectively of victims, of VAW and offenders, and integrated policies. It also establishes the creation of the Group of Experts on Action against Violence against Women and Domestic Violence (GREVIO). The convention "forces" MSs to implement the measures of the Convention by highlighting women's rights and their full enjoyment of a life free from violence. However, women remain passive actors of policies, often recalled as the victim in the whole text of the Convention, despite their empowerment and the cooperation with women's movements being 'encouraged.' Conceiving women as victims in laws and policies on gender-based violence has both advantages and disadvantages. On the one hand, emphasizing women as victims highlight the disproportionate harm they experience due to gender-based violence and reinforces the need for legal protection and support services (Renzetti, 2018). This victim-centered approach can help raise awareness, mobilize resources, and foster empathy and solidarity within society (Pettit & Lee, 2018). Moreover, recognizing women as victims can facilitate their access to justice, encourage reporting of incidents, and promote accountability for perpetrators (Heise, 1998). On the other hand, solely framing women as victims may perpetuate a narrative of vulnerability, reinforcing stereotypes and undermining their agency and resilience (Bacchi, 2012). This approach risks overlooking the diverse experiences of women, their capacity for resistance, and their potential roles as agents of change (Kelly et al., 2005). Furthermore, it may hinder efforts to address structural and systemic factors that contribute to gender-based violence, such as gender inequality and harmful social norms (Flood, 2011). Striking a balance between recognizing women as victims while also promoting their agency and empowerment is crucial for comprehensive and effective responses to gender-based violence. Thanks to the measures envisaged and the control of the GREVIO group, the Convention represents an instrument of control for the individual signatory states and the gold standard in regional and global efforts to counter GBVAW, despite the recent withdrawals by, for example, Turkey in 2021.[4]

Categories and thematic lines within CoE documents on VAW/GV/GBVAW

The three documents of the CoE show the evolution in the CoE treatment of the phenomenon of violence perpetrated against women.

One constant is evident in all the documents: women are increasingly treated as vulnerable subjects. However, there are a number of specifics in the texts, especially in the last and first documents where women's agency is fostered, although it is not specified how it can be encouraged.

The impositions that characterize the CoE strategies to deal with VAW/GBVAW in the 2002 recommendation, for example, on the role of media and images to be transmitted to the broader public, give way to the organization of a specific set of strategies and policies, such as the 4Ps approach of the Istanbul Convention of 2011 and the creation of GREVIO to monitor the phenomenon within the MSs that signed the Convention, among them the EU and individual countries, including Spain and Italy. In detail, Spain signed the Convention on May 11 of 2011 and ratified it on April 10 of 2014. In contrast, Italy signed it on September 27 of 2012, and ratified the Convention on August 1 of 2014. Lastly, as in the next paragraphs, the EU signed the Istanbul Convention in June 2017.

Finally, there are two main thematic lines that emerge from the analysis of these three CoE texts: 1. VAW is a widespread social issue: specific laws and policies are crucial to balance men-women power relations and counter VAW; 2. VAW needs to be tackled with the interconnected cooperation of nation-states, and gender mainstreaming approaches in policies are crucial to tackling its occurrences.

Figure 3.2. shows the main concept-driven and analytical categories that emerged from the analysis of the CoE documents, as well as the interrelation among them.

---

[4] For more information, see: https://www.coe.int/en/web/portal/-/secretary-general-responds-to-turkey-s-announced-withdrawal-from-the-istanbul-convention?fbclid=IwAR0i0G4MyFYwucr8LwExMcNqSuglbdhb_gHlC6DWK9xhtFufSe49gx5heFo

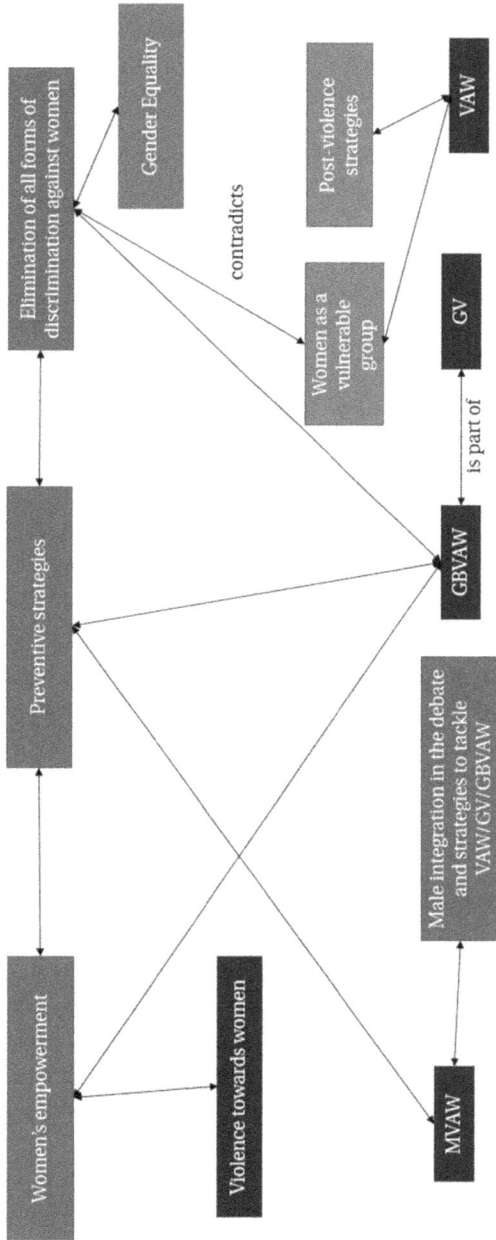

Fig. 3.2 CoE Documents on VAW/GV/ GBVAW: categories and thematic lines

Moreover, The selected documents from the Council of Europe provide insights into the organization's efforts to address and combat violence against women (VAW) and gender-based violence (GBV). An analysis of these documents reveals several key themes and perspectives:

Recognition of Imbalance of Power

The 2002 Recommendation on the Protection of Women against Violence acknowledges the existence of an imbalance of power between men and women, both in societal and familial contexts. It highlights the need to address this power imbalance as a root cause of violence against women.

Comprehensive Approaches

The documents emphasize the importance of comprehensive approaches to combating VAW and GBV. They advocate for active educational training, public awareness campaigns, and the involvement of men in ending violence. The Council of Europe encourages the implementation of national policies, the creation of controlling bodies, and the role of media and modern technologies in promoting non-stereotypical images of men and women.

Utopian Aspects

While the documents propose commendable measures, some aspects are seen as utopian or unrealistic. For instance, the expectation that media can entirely eliminate stereotypical images of men and women may be difficult to achieve, considering the influence of technology and the symbolic nature of violence. The lack of specificity regarding non-stereotypical views and the absence of individual interpretation raises concerns about potential censorship.

Women's Agency and Empowerment

The 2002 Recommendation and the 2011 Istanbul Convention recognize women's agency and empowerment in addressing VAW and GBV. They acknowledge that women can be agents of change and actively participate in ending the violence they experience. However, there are criticisms that these documents still primarily portray women as victims, which can reinforce stereotypes and overlook their diverse experiences, agency, and resilience.

International Cooperation

The Convention on Action against Trafficking in Human Beings (2005) and the Istanbul Convention (2011) emphasize the importance of international cooperation in addressing VAW and GBV. They aim to promote coordination among member states, with a focus on protecting women's rights and preventing violence in both public and private spaces.

Legal Frameworks and Monitoring

The Istanbul Convention (2011) establishes a legal framework for preventing and combating VAW and domestic violence. It introduces the concept of integrated policies and creates mechanisms such as the Group of Experts on Action against Violence against Women and Domestic Violence (GREVIO) to monitor and ensure implementation by member states.

Advantages and Disadvantages of Victim-Centered Approaches

Framing women as victims in laws and policies has advantages, such as raising awareness, mobilizing resources, and promoting accountability for perpetrators. However, solely portraying women as victims can reinforce stereotypes, undermine their agency, and hinder efforts to address underlying structural and systemic factors contributing to gender-based violence.

Withdrawals and Challenges

Despite the Istanbul Convention being considered a gold standard in regional and global efforts to counter GBV, there have been recent withdrawals by certain member states, such as Turkey, in 2021. This highlights the challenges and complexities in achieving full consensus and implementation across diverse national contexts.

Overall, the Council of Europe documents reflect a comprehensive and evolving approach to addressing VAW and GBV. They emphasize the need to address power imbalances, involve men, promote international cooperation, and establish legal frameworks while recognizing the importance of women's agency and empowerment. However, challenges remain in striking a balance between victim-centered approaches and promoting women's active roles as agents of change.

The next section of the chapter focuses on a regional body, the European Union. To understand the similarities, differences, and influences between the international and regional assets of Italy and Spain, the next paragraphs discuss the evolution of the EU documents on the phenomenon of VAW/GV/GBVAW from 1993 to 2015.

EU documents

Inside the conglomerate of states which creates the 28-year-old European Union (1992 Maastricht Treaty), different national policies and strategies have emerged in the fight and prevention of GBVAW and its gender perspective (Kantola, 2010). The European Union has acted as a facilitator of the implementation of some of the policies by proposing both non-binding and binding documents to address the issue (Montoya, 2013; Htun & Weldon, 2012). The influence of both the UN and of the Council of Europe in demanding the respect and the implementation, through acts and policies, of human rights has created a favorable environment for MSs to adopt a gender perspective and be actively present in the fight against GBVAW. A national level of analysis is still crucially preponderant. However, a regional set of policies within the European Union have characterized the evolution of the strategies used to deal with GBVAW, and new policies have intermingled the *global-local* scenario inside the European countries by challenging the traditional way of considering socially progressive policies toward specific components of civil society (Cimagalli, 2014; Lombardo & León, 2014).

Networking, social partnership relations, and educational approaches have emerged in the fight against GBVAW. They have integrated victim's support strategies in anti-violence centers by emphasizing the role played by workshops, educational meetings with perpetrators of violence, and awareness-raising campaigns within the European Union.[5]

The role of gendered policies has also been significant in some of the regions of the European Union. For example, it has been a tool for women's organizations in specific MSs, but also states who applied to enter the EU (i.e., Turkey) to influence national governments' policymaking on gender equality and women's rights and to ask as for specific funding measures (Eslen-Ziya, 2007). This impact has been – to some extent – valuable in the preventive strategies towards GBVAW, which have highlighted the hierarchical, androcentric state conception and have tried to foster gender equality by following, in some way, the universal caregiver model or ideal type (Fraser, 1997).

Regional measures (EU), as well as international norms (UN/CoE), have created a sort of facilitator process for governments' willingness to tackle GBVAW, fostering innovative and gender-attentive social progressive policies (Weldon & Htun, 2013). However, the lack of solidarity in the organization of states, despite some sort of inter-regional diffusion and the presence of the subsidiary principle, which delegates nation-states to mostly act independently, have hampered the diffusion of comprehensive policies to fight GBVAW in all the MSs. There have been both positive and negative effects based on the national context of single countries. Nevertheless, the EU has created a greater

---

[5] See: https://ec.europa.eu/info/policies/justice-and-fundamental-rights/gender-equality/ gender-based-violence/ending-gender-based-violence_en

civil society consciousness (Walby, 2004; Roth, 2008; Pavolini et al., 2015) to act together in the fight against GBVAW.

These 21 selected documents of the European Union's different bodies: EU Parliament,[6] Council of the EU,[7] EU Commission,[8] as in Table 3.3, show the evolution of the main EU documents on VAW/GV/GBVAW.

Table 3.3 European Union: documents on VAW/GV/GBVAW[9]

EUROPEAN UNION: DOCUMENTS ON VAW/GV/GBVAW			
YEAR	BODY	TITLE	TYPOLOGY
1995	EP	Resolution on the fourth World Conference on Women in Beijing: ' Equality, Development and Peace'	Resolution
	EC	Communication from the Commission to the Council and the European Parliament on Integrating Gender Issues in Development Cooperation Select: 5	Communication
1996	EC	Communication From The Commission "Incorporating Equal Opportunities For Women And Men Into All Community Policies And Activities"	Communication
	EP	Resolution on the follow-up to the Cairo International Conference on Population and Development	Resolution
	EC	Communication From The Commission To The Council And The European Parliament On Trafficking In Women For The Purpose Of Sexual Exploitation	Communication
	EP	Written Question No.1440/96 by Christine Oddy to the Commission. 'Stop violence against women'	Written Question
1997	EP	Resolution on the need to establish a European Union wide campaign for zero tolerance of violence against women	Resolution
	EP	Resolution on the Annual Report from the Commission: Equal opportunities for women and men in the European Union 1996	Resolution
	EC	Report from the Commission to the Council, the European Parliament, the Economic and Social Committee and the Committee of the Regions on the state of women's health in the European Community Select: 5	Report
1998	EC	Communication from the Commission on violence against children, young persons and women	Communication

[6] The EU Parliament is composed of 705 members. It is one of three legislative branches of the European Union and the EUs only directly elected institution.

[7] The Council of the European Union is the EU institution where ministers from the 28 EU countries meet to discuss, amend, and adopt laws, and coordinate policies.

[8] The EU Commission is the executive branch of the EU. It mainly proposes new EU laws and policies, monitors their implementation, and manages the EU budget.

[9] Tab. 3.3. shows the most relevant EU documents dealing wih GBVAW from 1993 to 2015. The table is the author's own output.

1999	EP	Resolution on violence against women and the Daphne Programme	Resolution
	EP	Resolution on the report from the Commission to the Council, the European Parliament, the Economic and Social Committee and the Committee of the Regions on the state of women's health in the European Community (COM(97)0224 C4-0333/97)	Resolution
2000	EP	European Parliament Resolution on women in decision-making	Resolution
	EC	Report from the Commission to the Council, the European Parliament, the Economic and Social Committee and the Committee of the Regions - Equal opportunities for women and men in the European Union - 1999	Report
2002	EC	Report from the Commission to the European Parliament and the Council on the Daphne Programme (2000-2003) - January 2002 (SEC(2002) 338) Select: 11	Report
2003	EP	European Parliament Resolution on violation of women's rights and EU international relations (2002/2286(INI))	Resolution
2004	EP, Council of the EU	Decision No 803/2004/EC of the European Parliament and of the Council of 21 April 2004 adopting a programme of Community action (2004 to 2008) to prevent and combat violence against children, young people and women and to protect victims and groups at risk (the Daphne II programme)	Decision
2007	EP, Council of the EU	Decision No 779/2007/EC of the European Parliament and of the Council of 20 June 2007 establishing for the period 2007-2013 a specific programme to prevent and combat violence against children, young people and women and to protect victims and groups at risk (Daphne III programme) as part of the General Programme Fundamental Rights and Justice	Decision
2009	EP	Elimination of violence against women European Parliament Resolution of 26 November 2009 on the elimination of violence against women	Resolution
2012	EP, Council of the EU and Council	Select: 1 establishing minimum standards on the rights, support and protection of victims of crime, and replacing Council Framework Decision 2001/220/JHA	Directive
2017	Council of the EU	Council Decision (EU) 2017/865 of 11 May 2017 on the signing, on behalf of the European Union, of the Council of Europe Convention on preventing and combating violence against women and domestic violence with regard to matters related to judicial cooperation in criminal matters	Decision

Analysis of selected documents

a) 1995, Resolution "Fourth World Conference on Women in Beijing: 'Equality, Development and Peace,'" EP

The main focus of the Resolution is the elimination of all forms of discrimination against women and the achievement of gender equality. The Resolution is intended to welcome the principles of the Beijing Declaration and to contextualize them within the EU. It is central to focus on the way those ideas and plans for action that were agreed upon in China were translated in Europe, specifically in the bodies of the European Union. In letter D of the Resolution, there is a clear statement on the role of the European Union as a vanguard regional authority that should serve as an example for other countries across the world in the matter of women's rights and the elimination of all forms of discrimination towards them. The preferred term is equality versus equity, which does not cover the idea of equal opportunities, therefore starting from different points, but it is still a first declaration of intent: "Equality between women and men is a vital precondition for the strengthening of democracy, development and improving the quality of life, not only in Europe." On page 38 of the document, there is a clear reference to women's rights since the EU: "Supports emphatically a woman's right to self-determination over her own body, including her reproductive and sexual rights" (p. 38). This document fosters the idea that gender discriminations are the basis of gender inequality and affect women disproportionally (Nayak & Suchland, 2006; York, 2011;). One of the key issues is, therefore, the focus on gender mainstreaming, which is also evident in the following 1995 Communication from the Council and the European Parliament on integrating gender issues in development cooperation.

b) 1995, Communication "Integrating Gender Issues in Development Cooperation," EC

The main idea of the document is to build a new partnership between women and men and to adopt a gender-sensitive development cooperation approach, transversal to EU issues, where development and sustainability are directly linked to women's empowerment and where the collaboration between the diverse groups of society is key in order to recognize and – henceforth – prevent any form of discrimination.

c) 1996, Communication "Incorporating Equal Opportunities for Women and Men into All Community Policies and Activities," EC

In 1996, with the Communication "Incorporating equal opportunities for women and men into all community policies and activities," the issue of equality between men and women is considered "a basic principle of democracy and respect for humankind" (p. 2) and, therefore, GBVAW is a human rights violation because it acts as a form of inequality between men and women. Measures to curb GBVAW are listed according to: "a) the organization and financing of public awareness campaigns concerning the problems of violence against women; b) medical and psychological assistance and other types of care for women who are victims of violence; c) the development or creation of programs aimed at providing training in this area for the legal and medical professions, social workers, teachers and the police" (p. 10). The only clear mention to preventive strategies refers to "formulate laws to prevent sexual tourism and the trafficking of persons, in particular the trafficking of women in prostitution networks" (p. 11). This document is key due to the reflection on the pressure exercised by the international community towards the EU and its MSs to provide a list of possible strategies to address VAW and the emphasis on including the gender perspective in its policies (Walby et al., 2017; Montoya; 2013; Kantola, 2006) planning and implementation, therefore avoiding any form of discrimination.

d)   1996, Resolution "Follow-up to the Cairo International Conference on Population and Development," EP

The Resolution "Follow-up to the Cairo International Conference on Population and Development," stresses the relevance of equality in society and the elimination of disparities and discriminations as a direct outcome of gender-related issues and roles (Nayak & Suchland, 2006). Therefore, this document – as the previous ones – presents a gender mainstreaming approach meaning where the focus on gender discrimination prevails over gender invisibility and over clustering women as one vulnerable part of the society as in the women's only approach (Walby et al., 2017). In the same Resolution, both women's rights as human rights and gender discrimination as the basis of violence perpetrated against women are clearly mentioned.

e)   1996, Communication "Trafficking in Women for The Purpose of Sexual Exploitation," EC

In this Communication, the emphasis is centered on a comprehensive framework of VAW with specific attention on sexual violence. Preventive strategies are envisioned and planned at an EU level and comprise: "support for information campaigns for raising public awareness of violence against women, as well as the exchange of information and of good practice in the fight against trafficking in women" (p. 18). The communication contemplates an EU framework and agenda to deal with sexual violence, and also in measuring appropriately any data and information to be compared cross-nationally. The Communication is important because it highlights the need to conflate data and best practices across states to reduce rates of VAW/GV.

f)   1996, Written Question "Stop violence against women,'" EP

The Written Question No.1440/96 by Christine Oddy (English politician) to the Commission. 'Stop violence against women' addresses two interconnected issues related to the promotion of gender equality by recalling the Beijing declaration and the necessity to raise awareness campaigns with an information campaign financed by the Commission and call for actions to single MSs, bearing in mind the lack of implementation following the June 1995 Madrid declaration on developing strategies to stop violence against women. It is interesting to note the urgency with which Oddy, turns to EP to ask for the implementation of the discursive practices of the conferences of previous years, a sign that VAW increasingly weighs on the agenda of individual states (Feci & Schettini, 2017; Montoya, 2013).

g)   1997, Resolution "Need to establish a European Union-wide campaign for zero tolerance of violence against women," EP

In the Resolution, the emerging argument is that both VAW and GV are human rights violations. In the preambulatory clauses in par. J, the Resolution stresses the importance of a cultural change by asserting that:

> "The majority of cases of abuse are not reported to the police, mainly due to the lack of proper legal, social and economic instruments to protect the victims, with the result that violence against women remains a largely hidden crime."

Therefore, the focus is also on how to make use of statistics properly and in a comparative perspective, as well as how to craft preventive strategies and policies to fight GBVAW. Men and women are treated as equal actors in the scenarios of violence, and cultural perceptions are challenged: "whereas men's violence against women is still surrounded by myths, such as domestic violence being a private matter or the idea that women's behaviors can be to blame for men's violence against them" (Preambulatory clause, par. N). VAW/GV/GBVAW are a cultural problem at the societal level since, as in the Resolution in operative clause number 2: "gender-based violence not only reflects unequal gender power relations in our society but also forms a formidable barrier to efforts to overcome inequality between women and men." The focus is not merely on women as a vulnerable part of society and as victims but goes further and highlights, for instance, "the importance of lifting the secrecy surrounding violence in society" (Operative clause, n. 3) beyond seeing violence as a private fact, thus also recalling the DEVAW. Strong agency and women's empowerment are also emerging categories in the Resolution that represents, as in operative clauses number 4 and 5, an extensive call upon member states to act to implement legislative measures. Best practices among MSs are also encouraged. In the Resolution, there is also a preponderant reference to VAW as an ecological model (Heise, 1998; Casique & Furegato, 2006) so that – ultimately – there is the provision of a "campaign to seek to alter attitudes in society so that zero tolerance of violence against women is achieved at the individual, collective and institutional level" (Operative clause, n. 39).

h)   1997, Resolution "Annual Report from the Commission: Equal opportunities for women and men in the European Union 1996," EP

The Resolution underlines the fight against gender-based discrimination. Gender violence as a paradigm is prevalent. However, flexibility in the choice of expressions used, mostly GV and VAW, is evident. Physical violence and other forms of violence are encompassed in the whole text. They all are considered a consequence of physical violence, thus valuable of less attention. The intention of the document is to acknowledge that "Whereas the concept of parity democracy between women and men should be put into effect in order to increase citizens' identification with the democratic process and political structures" (Section E), "a glossary of terminology in the field of equal opportunities" (Section 5) is fundamental. Finally, the Resolution "regrets the lack of attention paid in the Annual Report to the issue of violence against women, given that gender-based violence reflects the inequality between women and men in society" (Section 2). Thus, the Resolution is key in that it envisages the need for both research on the issue and the involvement of civil society.

i)   1997, Report "The state of women's health in the European Community," EC

The Report emphasizes GBVAW as an important women's health issue and a human rights concern. Domestic violence, rape, and sexual assault, as well as sexual harassment and stalking, are part of the report. VAW acts, especially domestic violence, are conceived as "social determinants which influence women's health within the context of evolving demographic and social trends" (p. 5). There are also plenty of references to the reasons behind acts of violence against women and its health concerns, as in this section:

> The European Women's Health Network, established in Vienna in 1994, included violence against women as one of six major health concerns. Although violence against women is known to cut across socio-economic, cultural, religious, and racial boundaries, there is concern that some groups of women, such as the elderly, migrants, and poor women, may be especially vulnerable. The causes of violence against women are unclear, but alcohol and drug abuse, poverty, and overcrowded conditions are factors known to exacerbate violent attacks on women. It has also been suggested that changes in society aimed at

improving the status of women (relative to men) may have contributed to increased assaults and sexual violence against them. (p. 115)

There is a reference to the way some MSs reacted and were interiorizing these new dispositions. For example, in 1992, in Spain, the number of reported cases of rape was 1599 (p.116), representing a higher number compared to other MSs. In this case, the data might be considered the reflection of the growing awareness of the issue from Spanish society more than the increase in cases of violence in the country.

j)   1998, Communication "Violence against children, young persons and women," EC

In the 1998 Communication "Violence against children, young persons and women," the main theoretical points of references are VAW and Violence towards women, where violence is considered a human rights violation. Domestic violence is often conceived as the most prevalent form of violence. The gender perspective and mainstreaming are the determinant factors that emerge from the text when discussing ways to tackle VAW. There is the disposition for community actions in the period 2000-2004: joint initiatives at an EU level among MSs, community institutions, and NGOs collaboration networks are considered crucial to address violence towards the different subjects the Resolution addresses. As for women as subjects, in the Resolution, the ecological model of violence prevails. The most used expression is "towards women." As already stated in the documents of the CoE, this expression considers more agency and empowerment on the women's side, which, finally, are seen as more than just victims. The communication places specific emphasis on the physical and mental health of the victims as well as on the need for substantial funds to help and assist them. It also fosters community action in the field as well as a subsidiarity principle, as in par. 5, and NGOs activities, namely the exchange of information, coordination and cooperation, the raising of public awareness, and the exchange of best practices. The communication also emphasizes the importance of preventive strategies. Finally, some of the specific objectives are to set up networks and assure the exchange of information, to coordinate and cooperate at an EU community level (Annex, p. 20-24), and, thus, the Daphne program on violence against children, young persons, and women.

k)   1999, Resolution "Violence against women and the Daphne Programme," EP

In the 1999 EU Parliament Resolution on violence against women and the Daphne Programme, the theoretical points of reference are VAW and GV, and in both cases, they are considered human rights violations. The text of the Resolution introduced the main definition of the phenomenon:

"Violence against young and adult women is taking place within the family, at the workplace, or in society and includes, inter alia, ill-treatment, battering, genital and sexual mutilation, incest, sexual harassment, sexual abuse, trafficking in women and rape." (Preambulatory clause, C)

GV is declined as a set of criminal offenses. The Resolution is also relevant because it calls upon MS to implement both legal measures to fight and prevent GBVAW but also envisages a coordinated approach among different departments, member states, and local, national, and international bodies, with an emphasis on shared information among MSs and cooperation.

l)   1999, Resolution "The state of women's health in the European Community," EP

The Resolution focuses on women's health in the European Community. In the preambulatory clauses, "Women's health status is also determined to a large extent by socioeconomic factors" (D). One aspect to ponder is that women are considered 'naïve' in the Resolution to the extent that they need to be 'informed': "whereas the disease and death rates among women may decrease considerably as soon as women are provided with adequate information on prevention and whereas women may also channel the information on to men." As with the focus on Domestic Violence "Calls on the Member States to make domestic violence against women, including rape within marriage and sexual mutilation, a criminal offence and to set up services to help women who are victims of this kind of violence" (Operative clause, n. 23). Again, the stress is on women as a vulnerable group instead of being on women's empowerment.

m)   2000, Resolution "Women in decision-making," EP

The Resolution emphasizes the balanced participation of women and men in the decision-making process. In the preambulatory clauses:

"Deeply regretting that women are major victims of human rights violations such as rape, sexual abuse, domestic violence, trafficking in human beings, etc., are under-represented on the judiciary and legislative bodies judging on the crimes mentioned and deciding on legal provisions, with the consequence that little or no priority is given to these crimes often resulting in the non-prosecution of offenders, even those who are known" (L) Moreover:

"Convinced that women holding decision-making positions on an equal footing with men is a necessary condition not only for successfully putting an end to inequalities, gender discrimination and violence against women but for the benefit of the functioning of society as a whole" (N), the Resolution results in a key moment in the process of proposing a more balanced participation of women and men at all levels, EU and MS. Thus, considering that violence and other forms of discrimination against women are factors which hamper achieving this goal. There is a prevalence of gender mainstreaming approach that triumphs over women's only, with gender having a broader meaning.

n) 2000, Report "Equal opportunities for women and men in the European Union (1999)," EC

"From domestic violence in the home to women's human rights overseas, a more ambitious co-ordination of equality actions would heighten visibility and impact and distill the monitoring of progress in gender equality" (p. 5) is how the Report on Equal Opportunities for Women and Men in the European Union envisions VAW/GV/GBVAW. It focuses on promoting awareness as a strategy to tackle GBVAW and increase gender equality. It shows and comments upon the data retrieved as, for example:

"Eurobarometer published the results of research into European attitudes on violence against women, one of the largest cross-national studies of its type. The study found that few Europeans claim to know any victim of violence, although they believe the problem is widespread. Contrary to research evidence, most Europeans believe that victims of violence are most at risk from strangers rather than people they already know" (p. 10).

It is worth noting how it goes against the main way GV/VAW is framed and the definition that descends from it. Violence perpetrated against one specific part of society has a gender component both when it is committed by strangers and by already known people.

o) 2002, Report "Daphne Programme (2000-2003)," EC

VAW, sexual violence and trafficking in women, and gender-based violence are the main topics that the Resolution mentions. Preventive policies, best practices, and strategies to contrast violence are addressed in the Resolution. There is the creation of the "Stop Programme"- for victims of both sexual and non-sexual forms of violence (children and women). Training modules for trainers on the prevention of violence are encouraged, and male domestic violence is also related to the lower economic status of women in society. The Resolution also intends to create a set of indicators for measuring VAW (p.20). There is one significant aspect worth recalling, which is: "a school-based project examined the impact of language/linguistic structures/insults on violence" (p. 22), which emphasizes how violence is considered and, at the same time, reflects the linguistic and cultural choices made at both the societal and individual levels (Eastel et al., 2012; Aksan, 2009).

p)   2003, Resolution "Violation of women's rights and EU international relations," EP

In the Resolution, there is a strong reference to Gender Violence:

"Aware that victims of violence are both women and men; however, international implementation of human rights in practice tends to take less into consideration violence against women, which stems from the unequal nature of the relations between men and women, which is a feature of most societies, and unacceptable references to culture and tradition" (preambulatory clause, C).

"Projects exclusively to women and to women's welfare and development" (p. 3), therefore social progressive policies are intended as antidiscrimination policies (Cimagalli, 2014) that must consider GV as an issue to both men and women and should question; therefore, gender unbalances to be deconstructed (Baker & Leicht, 2017; York, 2011).

q)   2004, Decision "Programme of Community action (2004 to 2008) to prevent and combat violence against children, young people and women and to protect victims and groups at risk (the Daphne II programme)," EP and Council of the EU

Decision No 803/2004/EC asserts that: "The effects of such violence are so widespread throughout the Community as to constitute a genuine health scourge and an obstacle to the enjoyment of safe, free and just citizenship" (p. 1). Among the objectives envisioned in the text, there are: 1. to support and encourage the exchange, adaptation and use of good practice for application in other contexts or geographical areas; 2. to study phenomena related to violence; 3. implement proven methods in the prevention of and protection from violence; 4. to support and encourage both non-governmental organizations (NGOs) and other entities/associations, including local authorities (at the competent level), active in the fight against violence to work together; 5. to develop educational packages on the prevention of violence and on positive treatment; 6. to develop and implement treatment programs for victims and people at risk, such as children and young people who witness domestic violence, on the one hand, and perpetrators on the other hand, with the aim of preventing violence; 7. to raise awareness and the level of understanding of violence and the prevention of violence against children, young people and women with the aim of promoting zero tolerance of violence, the provision of support to victims and groups at risk, and the reporting of incidences of violence.

This Decision is of paramount importance since it is perhaps the first time that at an EU level, regional policies are redefined to implement the concept of zero tolerance towards violence, using a gender mainstreaming approach through a measure that is binding on the MSs, including Spain and Italy.

r) **2007, Decision "Programme to prevent and combat violence against children, young people and women and to protect victims and groups at risk (Daphne III programme) as part of the General Programme Fundamental Rights and Justice (2007 to 2013)," EP and Council of the EU**

In Decision No 779/2007/EC, the attention is on how to prevent and combat violence against children, young people, and women, as well as to protect victims and groups at risk (Daphne III programme). Zero tolerance towards violence "to encouraging support for victims and the reporting of incidences of violence to the competent authorities" (p. 4) and "identifying and enhancing actions contributing to positive treatment of people at risk of violence, namely following an approach that encourages respect for them and promotes their well-being and self-fulfillment" (p. 4). The aim is at "studying phenomena related to violence and its impact, both on victims and on society as a whole, including the health-care, social and economic costs, in order to address the root causes of violence at all levels of society" (p. 4).

This Decision mirrors the previous decision of 2004 in many respects but adds that violence is a danger not only to individuals in an isolated context but to society. Therefore, it recognizes the importance of implementing policies that contain stronger and more contextualized measures based on the individual national contexts of the EU countries.

s) **2009, Resolution "Elimination of violence against women," EP**

The preferred expression of the EP Resolution is Men's violence against women or MVAW: "a structural and widespread problem throughout Europe and the world, a phenomenon affecting victims and perpetrators irrespective of age, education, income or social position, and is linked to the unequal distribution of power between women and men in our society" (Preambulatory clause, J). The Resolution highlights the possible reasons behind the persistence of GBVAW: "apart from economic dependence (which is often the case for women), important factors in female victims not reporting violence lie in the societal culture and representations suggesting that men's violence against women is a private matter or that women themselves are often to blame for such violence" (Preambulatory clause, R).

Therefore, the resolution is crucially relevant since the EU Parliament proposes "a view to encouraging a Europewide exchange of good practice;" (Operative clause, 25) to guarantee the right to assistance and support for all the victims of violence and as an EU framework MSs should abide by in a broader context of policies.

t)   2012, Directive "Minimum standards on the rights, support and protection of victims of crime," EP and Council of the EU and Council

This Directive asserts that all the forms of violence directed against a person because of that person's gender, gender identity, or gender expression or that affect someone of a particular gender disproportionately are understood as gender-based violence. According to the text of the document, violence may result in physical, sexual, emotional, or psychological harm or economic loss to the victim. Gender-based violence is, therefore, conceived to be a form of discrimination and a violation of the fundamental freedoms of the victim and includes violence in close relationships, sexual violence (including rape, sexual assault, and harassment), trafficking in human beings, slavery, and different forms of harmful practices, such as forced marriages, female genital mutilation, and so-called 'honor crimes.' Moreover, the Directive emphasizes that women victims of gender-based violence and their children often require special support and protection because of the elevated risk of secondary and repeated victimization, intimidation, and retaliation connected with such violence (p. 3,12). The Directive also focuses on how violence in close relationships is a serious – and often hidden – social problem which could cause systematic psychological and physical trauma with severe consequences since the offender is a person whom the victim should be able to trust. Victims of violence in close relationships may, therefore, need special protection measures, and, in this, the situation can be worse if the woman is dependent on the offender economically, socially, or as regards her right to residence (p.3, 18). In the document, significant attention is given to victims' protection, as follows: "Victims must have the right to: understand and to be understood during contact with an authority (for example the plain and simple language); receive information from the first contact with an authority; make a formal complaint and receive written acknowledgment; interpretation and translation (at least during interviews/questioning of the victim); receive information about the case's progress; access victim support services." In this Resolution, the focus is again on post-violence strategies more than preventive ones, but the gender mainstreaming approach prevails over women's only and gender invisibility ones, demonstrating that the issue's definition and strategies to tackle GBVAW have to consider how one part of the society has been treated differently and discriminated precisely because of its gender identity (Ngozi Adichie, 2014).

u) **2017, Decision "Signing on behalf of the European Union, of the Council of Europe Convention on preventing and combating violence against women and domestic violence with regard to matters related to judicial cooperation in criminal matters," Council of the EU**

The definition of the 2011 Istanbul Convention is part of the Regulation, and in 2017, there is the signing, on behalf of the European Union, of the Council of Europe Convention on preventing and combating violence against women and domestic violence with regard to matters related to judicial cooperation in criminal matters. The EU signed the Convention in June 2017. However, in this book's case studies for the next chapter, Spain and Italy – as single nation-states – have abided by the rules and principles of the Convention since 2014.

Categories and thematic lines within EU documents on VAW/GV/GBVAW

These 21 documents selected from the European Union's different bodies mainly address these two aspects:

1. VAW is "among the least punished crimes in the world": research, data collection, tools for better practices, and shared information are of paramount importance.

2. VAW/GB/GBVAW needs to be tackled with the interconnected cooperation of nation-states, and gender mainstreaming approaches in policies are crucial to tackling its occurrences.

The EU placed an increasing amount of attention on the elimination of all forms of discrimination against women as a first step to counter GBVAW, by therefore considering and asserting that VAW/GV/GBVAW is not – and never – a private issue, therefore following more the UN evolution of documents on the issue than that of the CoE, and finally by adopting a gender mainstreaming approach in dealing with GBVAW incidence in its MSs.

Figure 3.3 details the interconnections among categories (concept-driven and analytical) and the main issues that emerged from the analysis.

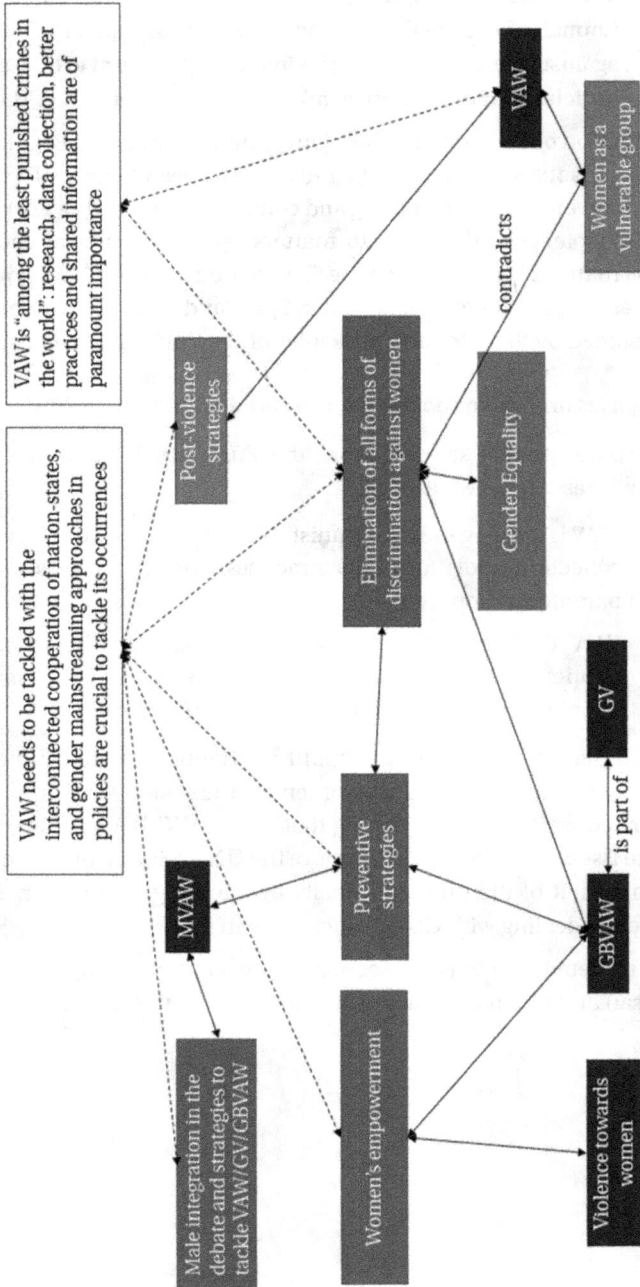

Fig. 3.3 EU Documents on VAW/GV/GBVAW: categories and thematic lines

There are also very interesting thematic lines that emerge from the analysis:

Gender Equality and Elimination of Discrimination toward the promotion of Women's Rights

The resolutions and communications emphasize the importance of achieving gender equality and eliminating all forms of discrimination against women. The EU recognizes that equality between women and men is crucial for strengthening democracy, development, and improving the quality of life. It highlights the need for integrating gender issues in all community policies and activities, ensuring equal opportunities for women and men, and promoting women's self-determination over their own bodies. Furthermore, the Beijing Declaration and its principles serve as a foundation for the EU's approach to gender equality. The EU aims to contextualize and implement the ideas and plans for action agreed upon at the Fourth World Conference on Women in Beijing. The EU supports women's rights as human rights and emphasizes the need to address gender-based violence, including domestic violence, rape, sexual assault, sexual harassment, and trafficking.

The Interconnectedness between Gender Mainstreaming and Preventive Strategies

Gender mainstreaming is a key strategy promoted by the EU to address gender inequalities and violence against women. It involves integrating a gender perspective into all policies and activities, recognizing the unequal power relations between women and men in society. The documents highlight the importance of preventive strategies, such as public awareness campaigns, medical and psychological assistance for victims, training for professionals, and laws to prevent violence and trafficking.

Human Rights Perspective on Women and Gender Issues

The EU frames violence against women as a human rights violation. It emphasizes that gender-based violence reflects unequal gender power relations and acts as a barrier to achieving equality between women and men. The EU calls for a cultural change and challenges societal myths and attitudes that perpetuate violence against women. It advocates for a zero-tolerance approach to violence and emphasizes the importance of lifting the secrecy surrounding violence in society.

Health and Socioeconomic Factors

The documents recognize the impact of violence against women on their physical and mental health. They highlight socioeconomic factors that contribute to violence, such as poverty, alcohol and drug abuse, and overcrowded conditions. The EU emphasizes the need for adequate information, prevention, and services to address women's health concerns and support victims of violence.

Collaboration and Coordination are the key

The EU emphasizes the importance of collaboration and coordination among member states, community institutions, and NGOs to address gender inequalities and violence against women effectively. It encourages the exchange of information, coordination of efforts, sharing of best practices, and the establishment of networks to combat violence and promote women's empowerment.

Women's Participation in Decision-making

The EU recognizes the underrepresentation of women in decision-making positions and calls for balanced participation of women and men in legislative and judiciary bodies. It acknowledges that women's perspectives are essential for effectively addressing crimes against women and developing appropriate legal provisions.

Overall, the selected documents demonstrate the EU's commitment to promoting gender equality, eliminating discrimination, and addressing violence against women. They highlight the importance of a comprehensive and coordinated approach that integrates a gender perspective into all policies and activities, challenges societal norms, and ensures the empowerment of women.

From private matter to shared responsibility: the evolution of international approaches to GBVAW

This chapter has explored the evolution of international, inter-regional, and regional documents on Gender-Based Violence Against Women (GBVAW), highlighting the diverse approaches taken by various organizations. It traces the progression from viewing GBVAW as a purely private issue to a problem that undermines equality between men and women up to the gender mainstreaming approach, which takes into account the "gender" variable within policies and does not consider women merely as vulnerable subjects and victims, but also as subjects with an agency. Regarding the relations among states, the evolving approach among the various bodies moves from the consideration of GBVAW as a problem to be dealt with at the national level, especially in the UN documents of the first years, to a greater emphasis, clear at a CoE level, and recently resumed – especially with the Daphne programs by the European Union – towards the sharing of best policy practices and an interconnected effort among MSs.

The evolution of the UN and CoE documents influenced the decisions and the legislative developments of the EU on GBVAW. For example, it was only in the 1990s, with the global awareness of the international community, that the EU started to play "a more active role" in preventing and fighting GBVAW (Montoya, 2013, p. 6). Consequentially, in terms of policies and shared practices, both narratives and practices on GBVAW in the frame of human rights violations have increased over the last two decades (Bodelón, 2013; Swantor., 2019). However, the implementation of these concepts is still lacking, and the disparity between narratives and practices/realities remains relevant. As Montoya (2013) asserts, for domestic policies to change international and regional variations are essential. Nevertheless, there should be an emphasis on how to connect the global to the local for tools and strategies to be effective. In this regard, the pivotal role of transnational advocacy in improving opportunities for change at the local level and combating GBVAW cannot be overstated.

Explicit legislation plays a crucial role in refining the legal systems' response to GBVAW, leaving no room for interpretation that might tolerate violence (Montoya, 2013, p. 7). Consequently, the following chapter will concentrate on Spain and Italy, examining their individual national-level approaches to GBVAW. Additionally, the chapter will provide a comparative perspective, highlighting the influence of international, inter-regional, and regional documents on these countries.

Chapter IV

Italian and Spanish laws
and policies on GBVAW

Summary: The evolution of the UN and CoE documents has influenced the decisions and the legislative developments of the EU on GBVAW. For example, it was only in the 1990s, with the global awareness of the international community, that the EU started to play "a more active role" in preventing and fighting GBVAW (Montoya, 2013, p.6). The role of explicit legislation is key to refining the legal systems' response to GBVAW since there is no space left for interpretation that may tolerate violence. (Montoya, 2013, p. 7). For this reason, this chapter focuses on Spain and Italy, considered separately at a national level and, later, in a comparative perspective by also pointing to the influence that those international, inter-regional, and regional documents have had on the individual countries.

Introduction

This chapter examines the laws and policies implemented at the national level in Italy and Spain, focusing on their individual evolution and comparing the two countries. The objective of this chapter is to underscore the role of nation-states in developing laws and policies to address Gender-Based Violence Against Women (GBVAW). By utilizing process tracing and conducting interviews in Spain and Italy, the chapter provides an in-depth analysis of the laws and policies implemented at the national level. It begins by discussing Italy's legislative framework and explores the overall level of government responsiveness (GR) observed in the country from 1993 to 2015. The Spanish case is then presented, following a similar structure as the analysis of Italy. Finally, the concluding paragraph highlights the significant role of both transnational and national movements in countering GBVAW.

Italy: selected laws and policies

The table below shows the main laws and policies adopted by Italy from 1993 to 2015. The laws and policies were selected according to their importance in the Italian system, their influence on the national and international debate, and the careful reconstruction of events that led to the approval of such laws and policies; therefore, the country Government's Responsiveness to GBVAW. The most relevant ones for this book are the following 12 laws and policies:

Table 4.1 Italy: laws and policies on VAW/GV/GBVAW (1993-2015)[1]

ITALY: LAWS AND POLICIES ON VAW/GV/GBVAW (1993-2015)		
YEAR	TITLE	TYPOLOGY
1996	Norms against sexual violence, n.66	Law
	Ministry of Equal Opportunities	Policy measure
1998	Urban Project I	Policy
2001	Measures against violence in family relationships, n.154	Law
2002	Urban Project II	Policy
2006	Helpline 1522	Policy measure
2008	National action plan against sexual violence	Policy
2009	Public security and the fight against sexual violence, as well as' in acts of persecution n. 38	Law
2011	National action plan on women, peace and security	Policy
2013 2013	Ratification and implementation of the Council of Europe Convention to prevent and combat violence against women, n.77	Law
	Security and fight against gender violence, as well as on civil protection and provincial administration, n. 119	Law
2015	National plan against sexual violence	Policy

Analysis of selected laws and policies

a)   1996, Law: "Norms against sexual violence" n. 66

The first Law that deserves attention in relation to the Italian case is the Law of February 15, 1996, n. 66 entitled: "Norms against sexual violence." The Law, which took twenty years to be approved by the Italian Parliament, focuses on sexual acts, eminently physical violence, and fits within an incredibly special socio-cultural framework which, in Italy, used to consider sexual crimes as crimes against morals and not against the person. The Law does not envisage any prevention tools. Aggravating sentences are introduced to combat sexual violence in the case of minors and in the case of family relations between the offender and the victim, hence as post-violence strategies. In the case of group sexual violence, all the participants are punished, even if they are only spectators, and have different punitive sentences. The focus of the Law is on violence as a physical phenomenon: sexual violence and group sexual violence. The victims are not clearly mentioned or clustered, despite minors being more often referred to in the law. It is, therefore, of crucial importance to discuss some details of the normative text that represents the beginning of the discourse on violence and the condemnation of rape on Italian territory (Lagostena Bassi et al., 1997). As previously mentioned, in the text of the Law,

---

[1] Tab. 4.1. shows the most relevant Italian laws and policies dealing wih GBVAW from 1993 to 2015. The table is the author's own output.

constant attention is paid to minors, while terms such as "gender" or "woman" are not mentioned. Nevertheless, the generality of such a document can be seen as a principle of discourse on issues that are more sectorial and for specific parts of civil society, not necessarily as a deliberate omission or lack of interest in the subjects of violence who are not minors. However, this is the most valuable document produced in Italy on sexual violence and, broadly, on VAW (Feci & Schettini, 2017). However, it lacks a detailed examination of the subjects and specific attention to women, as in the case, for instance of other European states, such as Spain (Valiente, 2005; García, 2016). This law is of paramount importance because it represents a watershed in the understanding and punishment of sexual offenses and violence committed against women, as it considers the abolition of crimes against morality and identifies acts of sexual violence as acts to be legally punished since they are acts against the person.

b) 1998, Urban Project I

The Urban project began in 1998 and initially included the participation of these cities: Venice, Catania, Rome, Naples, Palermo, Foggia, Lecce, Cosenza, and Reggio Calabria. The project had these main objectives: the identification of indicators for the identification of GBVAW/VAW environments at risk, in the family and outside of it; the definition of common protocols of intervention within the network of participating cities; the support to VAW shelters in individual cities through specific funds; and the collection of data for the creation of a database for the preparation of a manual for the design of interventions and anti-violence services.

The predisposition of this project in the country is especially important, even if it characterizes only some cities and seven out of nine cities are in the south of Italy, one in the center, and only Venice in the north of the country. The measures foreseen are only and exclusively of a post-violence nature, and there are no preventive measures. The project includes only victims and shelters that can accommodate women victims of violence. The desire to create a database for the analysis of the phenomenon is remarkably interesting but of little success at a local level and only considers women who seek refuge once they have already reported and are sheltered in the houses. The same year also saw the first survey funded by the National Agency for Statistics on sexual violence. However, the 1998 Urban Project was an emergency measure, and that will be a mantra in the country, as will often happen for other strategies of confrontation to GBVAW taken by Italy over the years.

c) 2001, Law: "Measures against violence in family relationships," n. 154

Law: "Measures against violence in family relationships" emphasizes domestic violence as happening inside the home. It introduced protection orders as part of the Penal Code and the removal of violent men from the family home. As for the theoretical points of reference in the analysis, the document presents significant proximity to the ecological approach of VAW (Casique & Furegato, 2006; Heise, 1998). However, compared to the 1996 Law, it is not only physical and sexual violence that merit consideration as Violence perpetrated against women. This Law comprises a wider spectrum of acts of violence committed against a woman. For instance, it refers to times when "the conduct of the spouse or other cohabitant causes serious harm to the physical or moral integrity or freedom of the other spouse or cohabitant" (Art. 2). Although different acts of persecution and violence are accounted for, the issue – conceptualized as an integral phenomenon with respect to the condition of the injured persons – is still not very attentive to the victims, mentioning them only once as women and children. It is interesting to note that the expulsion of the aggressor from the family home is foreseen to protect the safety of the injured person, but if the need for assistance is essential for work purposes, it is only considered a limitation. The safety and protection of the victim, or potential victim, seems, therefore, to overshadow job safety.

d)   2002, Urban Project II

Urban II follows the rules of the 1998 Project, but it is extended to other cities and has an emphasis on research and interviews conducted with social workers to understand how they receive cases of violence locally, with women and men on the perception of violence and the experiences of battered women in shelters. There are 26 Italian Urban cities involved in the 2002 project (Urban II): Bari, Brindisi, Cagliari, Carrara, Caserta, Catania, Catanzaro, Cosenza, Crotone, Foggia, Genoa, Lecce, Milan, Misterbianco, Mola di Bari, Naples, Palermo, Pescara, Rome, Reggio Calabria, Salerno, Siracusa, Taranto, Turin, Trieste, Venice. The prevalence of cities is always in the south of Italy, and the focus is always on measures for the victims (post-violence strategies), although the interviews also involve the perception of the phenomenon and the inclusion of the debate of the male audience: victims and aggressors are both subjects to deal with to contrast GBVAW.

e)   2006, Helpline 1522 and Arianna National Anti-Violence Network

In 2006, the Ministry for Equal Opportunities inaugurated the 1522 national call line for VAW victims and implemented the plan for the Arianna National Anti-Violence Network. It provides a national helpline service to women victims of violence through 1522. The project is in continuity with the Anti-Violence Network between Urban cities as a meeting place and connection between national and local instances for more effective planning of policies. The project involved the creation of an Arianna's Network that contained materials, studies, contacts, and periodically updated and integrated information. The measures envisaged by the Arianna National Anti-Violence Network and the creation of 1522 are of crucial importance for the country because they demonstrate the growing importance that the authorities and political parties gave to the phenomenon of male violence against women. However, like previous Italian laws and policies, the strategies remain post-violence ones, and the consideration of women is only as victims and vulnerable subjects. An interesting point, which was missing with the Urban projects, is the creation of common practices and the sharing of local experiences to integrate policies at the national level.

f)   2008, National action plan against sexual violence

This funding, which includes the allocation of support measures to victims of sexual and GV, as stated in the text of the official National Gazette, comes from the reception and pressure of EU and CoE recommendations, as well as the DEVAW of the United Nations. The measures envisioned to curb sexual and GV, and therefore with a possibility to be funded by the plan, are very general. However, unlike the laws and policies of previous years, there is a specific reference to preventive measures, with the provision of a national plan of action at both school and cultural levels (media and campaigns) and specific programs for operators who deal with cases of violence (in the social, legal and health sectors). In addition, there is another novel aspect, with the national plan foreseeing an exchange of best practices between the experiences of the Italian context and the European framework.

g)   2009, Law: "Public security and the fight against sexual violence, as well as' in acts of persecution," n. 38.

This Law contains urgent measures in the field of public safety and the fight against sexual violence, as well as 'in acts of persecution.' The law introduces a number of aggravating factors to the crimes of sexual violence and considers the crime of stalking (acts of persecution), and aims to counteract its occurrences. The law asserts that in situations where acts of persecution generate anxiety and fear for the safety of the person and of others, which will influence the behavior of daily life, the aggressor's imprisonment increases from six months to four years. If the harassment and acts of a persecutory nature derive from a legally separated or divorced former spouse, the penalty is increased. Aggravating penalties are also envisioned if those suffering are either minors or pregnant women. The insertion of the circumstance of an act, or a series of acts, of a violent nature between persons who were previously in a relationship, is considered but only if certified by marriage, hence an extremely strict conception of a couple's relationship, but still important. The recognition of certain behaviors represents, in many cases, the indicators that prevent the perpetration of violent acts, especially in a couple or intimate relationship. Only if the judge deems it right the person against whom she has been exposed is warned and ordered to use a conduct "in accordance with the law." The power of discernment resolution is intricately linked to the opinion of the judge who makes decisions about the correct behavior of the individual in society. Moreover, behaviors considered as excessive are also evaluated within relationships, highlighting that VAW is not a merely private matter; on the contrary: it is a public issue.

h) 2011, National action plan on women, peace, and security

The Plan incorporates the notion of zero tolerance towards sexual violence as enshrined in the UN and EU recent years' provisions. The Plan is also the direct result of Italy's participation as a rotating member of the UN Security Council for two years. Specifically, the Plan considers actions to prevent and combat VAW, understood as a violation of fundamental human rights as well as a social cost. In addition, the Plan commits to developing, on a national scale, information campaigns and training courses for all the relevant stakeholders on the issue of VAW and to implement an ad-hoc strategy as in the 2008 National Action Plan on Violence against Women (with a budget of 18 million euros).

The Plan is important because in addition to providing minimum standards of prevention and contrast VAW/GV, it aims to integrate and update the provisions on the subject in Italy, those relating, for example, to the Law of 1996 and envisages a consultation with the regulations and international and regional resolutions in a perspective of gender mainstreaming.

i) 2013, Law: "Ratification and implementation of the Council of Europe Convention to prevent and combat violence against women," n. 77

A crucial step within the Italian normative panorama, but in an intra-regional spirit, is the ratification and implementation of May 11, 2011, Istanbul Convention adopted by the CoE on preventing and combating violence against women and domestic violence. The ratification provides for a "full and complete implementation" of the Convention (Article 2), and in Article 4, in relation to the entry into force of the Convention, the law states that "it is mandatory for anyone to observe it and comply with the Law of the State" (Law June 27, 2013, n. 77., Art. 4). Observing the specificities of the CoE Convention, it is important to stress that the preamble establishes the condemnation of all forms of VAW and that it states that "the achievement of de jure and de facto gender equality is a key element in preventing violence against women" (Istanbul Convention, preamble), and this is a new topic for Italy, a new way to look at VAW/GV/GBVAW.

Moreover, considering that the aim of the Convention is "to create a Europe free of violence against women and domestic violence" (Istanbul Convention, preamble), the Convention also envisages the establishment of a specific monitoring mechanism that Italy has to implement. Article 3 shows the different definitions, which are useful to discern the issue in terms of women and violence, and introduces new definitions that become part of the Italian laws and policies on the matter. For instance, VAW is:

> "a violation of human rights and a form of discrimination against women and shall mean all acts of gender-based violence that involve or are likely to involve women in harm or suffering of a physical, sexual, psychological or economic nature, including threats of such acts, coercion or arbitrary deprivation of liberty, in public or private life" (Istanbul Convention, Article 3).

The Convention also explains the meaning of the word "gender," according to the roles that a given society considers appropriate, as they are socially constructed, and that of GBVAW that affects women simply because they are women, thus introducing and spreading these concepts in Italy.

This conversion into the Law of the CoE Convention of 2011 is of crucial importance. It represents the moment when Italy begins to address, more comprehensively and within official documents, the concept of gender. With this Law, new formulations of the phenomenon of violence perpetrated against women begin to arise, among them: GV, GBVAW, and MVAW, which will be taken up in subsequent years in national laws and policies and will characterize national debates on the matter.

j) 2013, Law: "Security and fight against gender violence, as well as on civil protection and provincial administration," n. 119

Law October 15, 2013, n. 119: "Conversion into Law, with amendments, of the decree Law" contains urgent provisions on the security and fight against gender violence, as well as on civil protection and provincial administration. In the title, the issue is framed as "Gender Violence." The text of the Law presents flexibility in the conceptualization of the phenomenon and in consideration of Gender Equality as fundamental in the achievement of a country free from GV/VAW/GBVAW. Among the strategies to address GV, the law mentions prevention and awareness-raising campaigns, as well as shared good practices and governance among different territorial administrations. It also focuses on education in schools and data collection to curb GV/VAW/GBVAW.

k) 2015, National plan against sexual violence

The Plan makes direct reference to the Istanbul Convention of 2011 and its reception in Italy by the Law of 2013. It respects all the premises and will of the Convention and has a particularly relevant aspect: the recovery of abusers through specific paths. Other lines of action include communication, education, training, risk assessment, rescue, and socio-occupational reintegration of women victims of violence. The Plan is comprehensive and has no gaps from the point of view of programming in accordance with the 4Ps approach: protection, prevention, and persecution, respectively, of victims, of VAW, and of offenders and integrated policies. It also provides for a system of monitoring and evaluation of good practices of multi-level governance, from local to national, and shared with the CoE.

Laws and policies on Gender-Based Violence Against Women in Italy (1993-2015): a broader analysis of actors involved, and definitions adopted through interviews

The moment Italy began to regulate VAW was in 1996: Law against sexual violence. There is no doubt about it, as this policy expert interviewee declares in this extract:

> Policies begin, I would say, since 1996, when it was sanctioned that VAW is a crime against the person and not against morality. That was the first point that marked a cultural shift. However, the challenge related to violence is also a structural challenge, we are not yet able to formulate policies that treat violence as a structural phenomenon, so our measures continue to be contingent.
>
> [Italian policy expert and researcher interviewed in May 2020]

As this policy expert asserts, policies have been characterized by the lack of structural and comprehensive policies on the issue. Therefore, Government Responsiveness in the country has always been based on one or more contingent events:

> Tracing the moments, we had laws and policies when, for some reason, something happened that stimulated and made known, I will say made imperative, to intervene. However, there has never been a work of structural planning and programming with respect to this phenomenon, so for example, in 2001, there was the law on violence in family relationships; in 2009, the anti-stalking law, that of Mara Carfagna[2] - as a result of the case of at a lawyer who had acid thrown in her face, or in 2011 we implemented the Istanbul Convention and in that year the law on feminicide. What I am implying is that what has been missing, and continues to be missing, is any form of structural, not contingent, intervention.
>
> [Italian policy expert and researcher interviewed in May 2020]

---

[2] Minister for Equal Opportunities in the fourth right-wing and conservative Berlusconi government (2008-2011).

In Italy, public policies on VAW started to have more echo with the Law on sexual violence of 66/1996 (Lagostena Bassi et al., 1997; Fondazione Nilde Iotti, 2019). However, the country still lacks a clear, contextualized national definition of VAW/GBVAW/GV and laws on the matter do not clearly mention subjects. Moreover, VAW/GBVAW/GV laws and policies present a prevalence of gender invisibility approach (Walby et al., 2017): there is a total lack of references to gender, except for the last couple of policies and Laws that integrates EU and CoE dispositions on the matter. The same happens with reference to VAW/GBVAW/GV. In the documents, equal opportunities between men and women are more frequently used than definitions of violence perpetrated against women, and the definitions are either used as synonymous or avoided in exchange, for instance, of sexual or domestic violence expressions. Here are some examples of the definitions used in Italy, according to the interviewees:

> When I started it was fashionable to talk about stalking, because the Parliament approved the law that considered it as a crime...
>
> [Italian activist and journalist, interviewed in May 2020]

> In my opinion the term GV is very important, but our media tend to pass it off as VAW, which creates a variety of problems because the focus is always on the victims and the discourse remains sterile and, hence, it is not understood why there is this problem...In my opinion the problem is a gender problem and there are power dynamics that lead to violence... we need, at societal level, to understand that the problem of violence is related to gender because there are power dynamics between men and women that should be dismantled ... so in my opinion starting to say gender violence would be a first step ...
>
> [Italian activist and journalist, interviewed in June 2020]

Until 2012, there is significant flexibility in conceptualizing the phenomenon. Since 2013, there is a clear legislation on GBVAW/VAW. Nevertheless, the subjects are not explicitly mentioned in the documents either. An integral Law capable of preventing and combating the phenomenon of male violence against women is still missing. As for national plans, they start to appear in 2008, but the focus continues to be only on victims, with any preventive measures being scarcely introduced.

Since 2013, there has been a remarkable increase in national plans and policy measures, largely influenced by the European Union at a regional level. This influence can be seen through various resolutions such as those related to Daphne programs and zero tolerance campaigns. Furthermore, the presidency of the European Council, particularly exemplified by the Spanish government under Zapatero, has played a significant role as both an accelerator and a source of best practices for the region.

A pivotal moment in this progression was the comprehensive national plan of 2015. This plan incorporated all the recommendations outlined in the 2011 Istanbul Convention from the Council of Europe. Without the influence of the aforementioned EU resolutions and the specific Istanbul Convention, it would have been considerably more challenging for the country to achieve its goals, especially within such a short timeframe. The Istanbul Convention has had consequences and has made clear aspects that the country cannot ignore, not anymore.

[Italian activist and journalist, interviewed in May 2020]

Transnational advocacy has forced those boundaries that, within the Italian feminism, had prevented laws and policies evolution. Starting with Beijing 1995, this aspect and comparison with practices of other countries has certainly produced a positive forcing in the government responsiveness of Italy and its national dynamics.

[Italian activist and researcher, interviewed in June 2020]

Istanbul has been of pivotal importance, even more than the other Resolutions and Conventions, also because it came at a time when the national level was more ready to accept some indications from the outside. Even if in the 90s, the national level was quite active, the years 1993-1995 were very important because the international documents made Italy get a move on in the following years, let's say, and also because in those years, the feminist movements were strong and listened to, so useful exchange for laws and policies development, while then in the 2000s there was a moment of "tranquility" also for the changes of government and here, until Istanbul, which is now a new wave of movements who demands more attention on the issue. Italy immediately ratified the Istanbul Convention – at the time, the government was in favor – and, then, it is also thanks to the Convention that the national plan of action was created and is based on the 4 Ps approach of the Istanbul Convention... At the normative level, it is fundamental, while at the practical level, as in the GREVIO report, there are many critical issues, also due to regional variability ... but I must say that at all levels, and also for movements and associations, having an international document like the Istanbul Convention and a binding one is essential to assert their expertise and experience; and to the policies creation and to improve the dialogue with institutions... Moreover, the work of GREVIO is especially useful since it sheds light on the critical issues and the functionality and shadow relationships of the various associations. In my opinion is giving a lot of value to how public administrations should react and also recognizing the role of anti-violence centers and the grassroots on the ground, so the Convention is useful for both public administrations for all levels to regulate in terms of laws and policies and for bottom-up associations, an aspect that is in line with European Resolutions and Directives.

[Italian policy expert and researcher interviewed in June 2020]

Italy receives the influence of international bodies and has transnationally driven reforms (Montoya, 2013), but the national political change in governments is also important:

I am ruthlessly honest, and I tell you that the political rise of a party like the Northern League (extreme right) has made the situation much worse in the sense of the difference, even in the initiatives to sensibilize the population that were made by the center-left administrations and the way in which the theme has been, or rather has not been, treated by the right parties, it happened to me in conferences and public meeting with that extreme right party. I have seen their total disinterest, comments for which they were losing their time ...

[Italian activist and journalist, interviewed in May 2020]

Based on my experience, and this, then, precisely remains anonymous, policies change a bit depending on who is in power

[Italian policy expert and researcher interviewed in June 2020]

The relevance of the political parties in power to address GBVAW in terms of laws and policies happens for a reason, as in the words of one of the respondents:

In my opinion, there is a lack of connection between politics and civil society, in part because there is this disconnection between feminism and people in politics who rarely identify with the demands of feminism ... for example, I believe that Laura Boldrini[3] has done a lot from the point of view of communicating with civil society, I believe that there is a lack of involvement of people who see themselves in feminism and have this kind of approach. Therefore, there is lack of contact with movements of intersectional feminism in politics of transmission at the political level... Briefly, feminists are missing in politics, and there is a lack of debate among those who have been dealing with GBVAW for a long time (workers in anti-violence centers, NGOs).

[Italian activist and journalist, interviewed in June 2020]

---

[3] Italian left-wing politician and President of the Chamber of Deputies from 2013 to 2016.

The influence of international documents and the way governments respond to GBVAW is also reflected in the widespread flexibility concerning the use of the terms GV and VAW. For instance, the first formula emerged only in the last 5 or 6 years, especially because of the action of international and regional bodies, as this interviewee suggests:

> Today the role of these intermediate bodies remains central and strategic in stimulating the government to respond to the indications that come to us from the European level and the Council of Europe, even on definitions.
>
> [Italian policy expert and researcher interviewed in May 2020]

GVAW as an expression is even more recent and often subsumes that of MVAW, here are some of the reasons behind the choice of one or the other definition.

> MVAW means mentioning the perpetrators and not just the victims, therefore men. Second, it is better to use the term "against" women and not "on" women in order not to represent an idea of inferiority and victimization of women. I am not opposed to the use of the term GV because I believe that MVAW has a close connection with transphobic, homophobic, etc. violence, i.e., it is true that MVAW is part of a system of construction of gender order.
>
> [Italian activist and researcher interviewed in June 2020]

GBVAW is not a form of deviance but:

> GV is always a device of reproduction and restoration of these power relations, it also means to recognize that violence is not a form of deviance and disorder, but it is a form of reproduction of this order, but at the same time we cannot address the issue of GV only in an emancipationist and egalitarian perspective, linked to the field of rights and women. The field of violence calls into question the imaginary, the symbolic, the sexual representations, the expectations, the construction of gender models in their complexity and, therefore, to crush it only to a reparative or egalitarian normative approach would be reductive.
>
> [Italian activist and researcher interviewed in June 2020]

> Violence is the extreme representation and consequence of discrimination... violence is a system not a piece, they are integrated policies, so if we do not make integrated policies, everything is relative.
>
> [Italian chairwoman of an association dealing with GBVAW and member of international organizations on the subject, interviewed in July 2020]

Echoing the words of the previous excerpt on integrated policies, the attention the country has given to the issue has been lacking and distracted, as another interviewee reminds us:

> I believe that Italy has always been a distracted country! For example, there is a distraction on the government's side, at least within the Ministry of Education, should emphasize the content of the school curricula and reserve a space for these issues, recognizing their importance because otherwise we will have no memory and at this point, it will become difficult for us to interact with the levels of government and ask for certain things, support certain requests. The distraction has always been there, and that is why the path of women in our country has always been a difficult path, and it is no coincidence that several authors have spoken of the invisible citizenship of women, therefore. An incomplete path, unfinished citizenship, which suggest that this path is not complete, and the attention of governments has always been scarce ... I actually believe that when we talk about these issues, we should refer to another level, that of power, and when we talk about power there is no color in the sense that there is no side, there are those who wanted to use the discourse of women to make it become a way to gain more votes, so they are used instrumentally, however for the important positions we meet very few female figures... as if there was no room for women in these areas ... so in my opinion, I do not see this attention to women and violence perpetrated against them, certainly when we see the governments of the left this attention is a bit greater, but still ...
>
> [Italian policy expert and researcher interviewed in May 2020]

Finally, this is how GR and policy creation occur in Italy:

> In Italy, above all, the network of anti-violence centers has been the subject that put more pressure on the institutions. For some years, a place where this happened was the national anti-violence plan in which there are all associations, representatives of the anti-violence centers, there are regions and ministries, that is the place of interaction between civil society and institutions in which policies are urged, but also monitor policies are envisaged, as well as the assessments on the effectiveness of actions implemented.
>
> [Italian activist and researcher interviewed in June 2020]

However, without the push of transnational advocacy, both in terms of documents to be integrated into the national legal apparatus, continues this respondent and others that were interviewed, as well as the support of some international resolutions for the purposes of the struggles and demands of women's and feminists movements, Italy would not have witnessed this GR on the matter, from 1995 onwards, with a pause due to changes of government in the early 2000s, and with a noteworthy push in the last decade of the twenty-first century.

Several themes emerge from the interviews conducted with policy experts, activists, and researchers.

Lack of structural and comprehensive policies

According to the policy expert, Italy's approach to GBVAW has been characterized by a lack of structural planning and programming. The policies implemented have been contingent, responding to specific events rather than addressing violence as a structural phenomenon. This highlights the need for comprehensive and long-term strategies to combat VAW effectively.

Historical development of policies

The interviews shed light on the key moments in Italy's journey towards regulating VAW. The first significant milestone was the 1996 Law against sexual violence, which marked a cultural shift by recognizing VAW as a crime against the person rather than against morality. Subsequent laws and policies were enacted in response to specific incidents, such as the anti-stalking law in 2009 and the law on feminicide in 2011. These contingent events shaped the government's responsiveness to the issue.

Gender invisibility approach

The analysis points out that Italian VAW laws and policies have predominantly lacked a gender-focused approach. The documents often use terms like "equal opportunities" instead of explicitly addressing violence perpetrated against women. This gender invisibility approach undermines the recognition of power dynamics and the gendered nature of violence. However, recent policies and laws have started integrating EU and Council of Europe dispositions, reflecting progress in this regard.

Influence of international bodies

Transnational advocacy and the influence of international bodies, such as the Beijing Conference and the Istanbul Convention, have played a pivotal role in shaping Italy's response to VAW. These international documents have prompted changes in policies and provided guidelines for addressing the issue. The Istanbul Convention, in particular, has been instrumental in the creation of the national plan of action and has highlighted critical issues that need to be addressed.

Political factors

The political landscape in Italy has influenced the government's approach to GBVAW. Changes in political parties and their priorities have had implications for policies and initiatives. The interviewees highlight the disconnection between politics and civil society, with a lack of involvement of feminist voices in policymaking. The rise of right-wing parties is seen as detrimental to the progress made by center-left administrations in raising awareness and addressing GBVAW.

Definitions and terminology

The choice of terminology to describe VAW is discussed in the interviews. The terms "GV" (gender violence) and "MVAW" (male violence against women) are considered important, but there is variation in their usage and preference. The interviews emphasize the need to recognize violence as a system that reproduces power relations, going beyond a purely normative or egalitarian approach.

Incomplete attention and distracted approach

The analysis suggests that Italy has historically had a distracted approach to addressing VAW. Governments have shown limited attention to the issue, and the involvement of women in positions of power has been inadequate. The lack of connection between politics and civil society, particularly with feminist movements and anti-violence centers, has hindered the development of effective policies.

Role of anti-violence centers and civil society

The network of anti-violence centers in Italy has played a crucial role in pressuring institutions and advocating for policies to address VAW. The national anti-violence plan serves as a platform for interaction between civil society and institutions, urging the formulation of policies, monitoring their implementation, and assessing their effectiveness.

To conclude, the analysis highlights the need for Italy to adopt a more structural and comprehensive approach to addressing VAW. It emphasizes the importance of integrating a gender-focused perspective, drawing from international frameworks, involving feminist voices in policymaking, and fostering collaboration between civil society and institutions.

Spain: selected laws and policies

The table below shows the main laws and policies adopted by Spain from 1993 to 2015. As for the Italian case, the laws and policies were chosen by looking at the importance they have in the national system, the influence they have had on the national and international debate, and a careful reconstruction of events that led to the approval of such laws and policies, therefore the Spanish Government Responsiveness to GBVAW. These are the 12 most relevant ones for the Spanish case:

Table 4.2 Spain: laws and policies on VAW/GV/GBVAW (1993-2015)[4]

YEAR	TITLE	TYPOLOGY
	SPAIN: LAWS AND POLICIES ON VAW/GV/GBVAW (1993-2015)	
1995	Law, 23 november, which amends the Penal Code, 10/1995	Law
	Law 35/1995, of December 11, on Aid and Assistance for Victims of Violent Crimes and against Sexual Freedom	Law
1998	First Action Plan against domestic violence	Policy
2003	Protection Order for Domestic Violence Victims, 27/2003	Law
2004	Comprehensive protection measures against gender violence (VioGen). 1/2004	Law
	Secretary General for Equality Policies	Policy measure
2005	Government Delegate against VAW	Policy measure
2007	Helpline 016	Policy measure
	National plan for awareness and prevention of gender violence	Policy measure
2008	Establishment of the Ministry of Equality	Policy measure
2013	National Strategy for the Eradication of Violence against Women (2013-2016)	Policy
2015	Law 1/2015, of March 30, which amends the Penal Code.	Law

Analysis of laws and policies

a)   1995, Law, which amends the Penal Code, 10/1995

This Law, which amends the Penal Code previously in force – in 1973– has interesting aspects due to the protection of victims of physical and sexual violence. In detail, the reformed Penal Code, specifically Article 153, includes physical domestic violence as a crime against the health and physical integrity of the victim. Furthermore, the Code provides for both punishment of the aggressor and protection of the victim. What the amendment produces as a change is an increase in the penalty to 3 years.

However, these changes in the Penal Code are extraordinarily little, and, for instance, one of the shortcomings of the 1995 Penal Code was the regulation of family violence initially only as physical abuse, something that will change in

---

[4] Tab. 4.2. shows the most relevant Spanish laws and policies dealing wih GBVAW from 1993 to 2015. The table is the author's own output.

the following Laws, plans of actions (1998, among others) and amendments of the Criminal Code, for example, that of 2015.

b) 1995, Law: "Aid and Assistance for Victims of Violent Crimes and against Sexual Freedom," 35/1995

The Law pays specific attention to re-insert victims of violent acts into the social context, especially by means of economic compensation. There is no reference to preventive strategies but only to ex-post strategies. The Law regulates access to a system of public aid for the direct and indirect victims of violent crimes, which considers only to be death, serious body injury, or severe damage to physical or mental health. Moreover, and this is a new aspect that was not considered in the previous documents, the Law also provides that victims of crimes against sexual freedom, even if perpetrated without violence, have access to this form of assistance.

c) 1998, First Action Plan against domestic violence

This first National Plan against Domestic Violence is approved by the right-wing conservative party in power at the time: the People's Party. The Plan is, more than anything else, the result of the protests that took place in the country following the feminicide of Ana Orantes in 1997. The event made the issue of VAW/GV an issue to be prioritized in national politics (Roggeband, 2012; Garcia, 2016).

The Plan is, therefore, fundamental for several reasons: it expands the measures aimed at countering the phenomenon of violence, and it includes preventive measures, education, and training. Furthermore, it is thanks to this Plan that politicians begin the discussion in the Spanish Parliament on an integral and organic law on the protection and prevention of VAW/GV; this process will culminate in the 2003 Protection Order for victims of domestic violence and in the 2004 Law against Gender Violence.

d) 2003, Law: "Protection Order for Domestic Violence Victims," 27/2003

The Protection Order for Domestic Violence Victims stipulates that the victims of domestic violence should obtain a comprehensive protection status that includes civil, criminal, welfare, and social protection measures. This Law, approved during the campaign for national elections by the conservative party, represents a moment of change that will lead the parliamentary debates to continue and the political parties to unanimously approve the Organic Law that regulates gender violence at the national level the following year. The importance of this law is in the integrality of the protection that is granted to victims of violence and the priority that the question of violence is taking in those years in the country, but it is also the result of the pressure of international documents. It is the moment in which Spain predates international and EU efforts on the matter (Montoya, 2013), especially those of the CoE, as clearly stated in the text of the law. Furthermore, this law on the protection order for victims of domestic violence will be, along with the 2004 Law, one of Spain's most extensive policies on the subject and will also be proposed as a model for other European countries during the Spanish presidency of the European Council, which occurred during the socialist government of the PSOE of José Luis Rodríguez Zapatero.

e)   **2004, Law: "Comprehensive protection measures against gender violence," 1/2004, and**

f)   **2004, Secretariat General for Equality Policies and**

g)   **2005, Government Delegate against VAW**

VioGen is the most relevant Spanish Organic Law on integrated protective measures against gender-based violence. The Law passed during the left-wing government of Zapatero (2004-2011) represents the beginning of extensive policy reform on the subject. This specific Law is the result of the dialogue between the parties present in the Parliament, at that time, Spain is still predominantly bipartisan with the conservative PP and the socialist PSOE, and women's and feminist movements (García, 2016).

The Law uses the expression GV but does not consider other subjects if not women, and the violence regulated within the law refers only to that between couples or ex-couples, therefore, mainly domestic violence. This definition has led to many debates and criticisms from both feminist and women's movements as it is considered inadequate to cover cases of GV in their entirety, where GV means violence perpetrated against a subject for gender reasons. In addition, the definition adopted by the law, which comes from the pressure of the PP to achieve the approval of the law unanimously, is a problem for the collection of statistical data because it does not give a real picture of the incidence of VG, but only of domestic violence.

However, VioGen is of crucial importance in many respects: it introduces a *Juzgados de Violencia sobre la Mujer* [Courts of Violence against Women], specifically to deal only with GV/VAW/GBVAW cases and *Fiscalía contra la violencia sobre la mujer* [Prosecutor's Office against Violence against Women]. VioGen is, also, an integral law that specifically legislates on this matter, unprecedented in European contexts and first in the country's history, thus defining that GV/VAW was an urgent issue that needed the attention and intervention of institutions, with it leading to a continuous modification of the protection of victims and prevention of GBVAW through specific measures, such as the creation of two women's policy agencies: the Secretary-General for Equality Policies in 2004 and the Government Delegate against VAW in 2005, that will adopt measures and public policies to counteract GV/VAW/GBVAW in the years to come.

h)   **2007, Helpline 016 and**

i)   **2007, National Plan for Awareness and Prevention of gender violence and**

j)   **2008, Establishment of the Ministry of Equality**

With the creation of the two women's agencies and the 2004 Law, the Zapatero government continued the GR on the subject and financed the helpline for victims of violence, a service that is still in force today and works in several languages: along with the National Plan for awareness and prevention of GV. The latter also includes preventive measures. Among its priorities there is the creation of specific training services for professionals in sectors ranging from justice, health, security services, and labor and social assistance; there is also a reference to programs that propose measures that respect the principles of gender equality in schools (starting from elementary school), and finally, the creation of reintegration services for victims, as well as for the aggressors. In 2008, the Secretary-General for Equality Policies became a fully-fledged public policy agency at a ministerial level, which shows the importance that these issues are assuming in the country.

k)   **2013, National Strategy for the Eradication of Violence against Women (2013-2016)**

It is one of the cornerstones of the government's political project to address GV and VAW. The strategy consists of four main objectives: breaking the silence that is complicit in violence; improvement of the institutional response; more attention to minors and women especially vulnerable to gender violence; visibility and attention to other forms of VAW. This strategy aims at both GV against multiple subjects and VAW, including new forms of physical violence such as trafficking and genital mutilation, forced marriages, and online forms of GV. Moreover, there is the principle of zero tolerance towards any form of gender-based violence as established in this tagline: *Ante el maltratador, tolerancia cero* [Zero tolerance for abusers].

l)   **2015, Law, which amends the 1995 Penal Code, 1/2015**

This law addresses the victims of GV and trafficking in human beings. It has some interesting features; for example, it incorporates gender as a reason for discrimination as an aggravating circumstance. It also focuses on the aggressors as it prohibits them from approaching the victim and obliges them to participate in equal treatment and non-discrimination programs. Furthermore, it provides that when the crimes are related to gender violence, no complaint is required for prosecution. In addition, the law introduces new criminal offenses related to GV: the crime of harassment or stalking (Article 172); the crime of "cyberstalking" (paragraph 7 of Article 197). Moreover, as the preferred theoretical framework adopted in the Law is the one of GV (Taylor & Jasinski, 2011; York, 2011; Nayak & Suchland, 2006), the documents mention gender reasons among the motives that lead to committing violence against a group or a specific person (Article 510). This law already shows a difference from the conceptualization of the GV as in the VioGen of 2004 and a total alignment with the provisions of the CoE 2011, but also the UN and EU Resolutions and documents.

Laws and policies on Gender-Based Violence Against Women in Spain (1993-2015): a broader analysis of the actors involved, and definitions adopted through interviews

The evolution of the laws and policies in Spain is remarkably interesting and is branded by a sort of acceleration of the laws and policies since the transition and establishment of democracy (1975-1978) until the period considered in this chapter. To understand how Spain considers GV/VAW/GBVAW, the definition according to the Spanish government is of crucial importance and takes into consideration the VioGen Organic Law of 2004, as well as the new dispositions on the matter of 2013 and 2015:

> Gender violence has been an invisible phenomenon for decades, being one of the clearest manifestations of inequality, subordination, and power relations of men over women. The verification of the existence of this situation will mark a turning point in the legal and social consideration of women's rights and freedom.[5]

This definition and laws approved since the end of the PP rule in 2003 and the beginning of the socialist government of Zapatero demonstrate that there is a prevalence of the gender mainstreaming approach, and hence the idea that VG is a result of gender discrimination and is linked to the lack of Gender Equality, but is also a mechanism to maintain control over women, as in the following extract:

> Violence (VG/VAW/GBVAW), for me is not only the manifestation of discrimination but it is also a mechanism, an instrument, the vehicle used by the patriarchy to maintain our discrimination and ensure that

---

[5] In Spanish (original): *La violencia de género se ha constituido como un fenómeno invisible durante décadas, siendo una de las manifestaciones más claras de la desigualdad, subordinación y de las relaciones de poder de los hombres sobre las mujeres. La constatación de la existencia de esta situación, marcará un antes y un después en la consideración legal y social de los derechos y libertades de las mujeres.* For more information, see: http://www.violenciagenero.igualdad.mpr.gob.es/definicion/home.htm

nothing changes: to preserve the status quo. It is precisely when we break roles that we resort to Violencia(s) Machista(s), and I realized that Violencia(s) Machista(s), or Gender Violence, as we want to call it, is a "patata caliente (tar baby)" as we say here in Spain, that is to say, it has many ramifications, it is a topic that covers so many issues that we really keep chopping it up, making entries to the subject but, really, it is not enough...

[Spanish policy expert and researcher interviewed in March 2020]

From the statements in the excerpt above, and as seen in the analysis of the selected laws and policies for the period (1993-2015), the preferred way to refer to the phenomenon in Spain, in the laws and policies, and for the movements is either GV since:

It is convenient to talk about gender violence because it is not only against women, but also against everything that is not male.

[Spanish feminist activist interviewed in April 2020]

In Spain, at a legislative level, when we talk about Gender Violence, we refer to violence in a couple or former couple and between men and women, the reference is to the 2004 VioGen law.

[Spanish member of a national public administration and policy expert interviewed in February 2020]

For this reason, in Spain, there are other aspects to consider when using an appropriate definition, and the reasons behind it are clearly explained in this extract:

It all started in 2004, which was an achievement of the feminists who managed to use the term Gender Violence and to make it clear that it was a structural problem, not of women who had been unlucky: a societal problem, a structural one...but the law for me made the worst mistake: it understood GV as exercised by partner or former partner but, let's see, if it is a structural problem, how can it be limited to these cases?... Hence the term GV poses problems if we refer to what the law of 2004 says, and it is true that the cruelest violence is domestic, some authors say that patriarchal violence is the most lethal and women die mostly at home, but it is not comprehensive... then we started to talk about Violencia(s) Machista(s) because in Spain there are people who identify GV only as that which occurs in the couple or ex-partner. Moreover, using the term GV also makes invisible who is the aggressor and who is the victim ... then gender is not enough to explain this kind of power of men toward women.

[Spanish policy expert and researcher interviewed in March 2020]

Another viable option is to use the expression Violencia(s) machista(s) because:

.... therefore when we use the expression Violencia(s) Machista(s), we are talking about men over women and the plural is preferable because there are many areas of application: at work, at the institutional level, in hospitals, cultural violence, symbolic, video ads and so on, and also many modes of application, it is much more than physical violence is psychological violence and then sexual violence even in the couple, to economic violence in the couple, so there are many areas and many modes of implementation: with Violencia(s) Machista(s) the description of the phenomenon is more defined.

...For me, Violencia(s) Machista(s) is a problem of men that women suffer, and I think that part of what is failing is that we are not focusing the problem on them, we are focusing mainly on women, on the effects, on the victims. It would be interesting to involve men, ask them, that is, if they consider that women are equal, and you know the answer is obviously "no."

[Spanish policy expert and researcher interviewed in March 2020]

Violencia(s) Machista(s) because they (the movements) understood that they explained more about the root of the problem... Because they are killing us (women), because there is violence, because we live in a macho society. So, we understand that by talking about machismo, we are better situating the root of the problem. We do not just talk about the victims, but we talk about the problem comprehensively. It is like a focus on what the problem is. The problem is the macho society. But this expression is used by the movements and then, because at the institutional level, Podemos has also used it.

[Spanish researcher, feminist activist and politician interviewed in March 2020]

The latest wave of feminism now wants to put the emphasis on the aggressors as well, on who is also guilty and not only the victim, and that is why we started to talk about GV, and it fits more in the Spanish terminology and also the media that refused a little bit to use the gender terminology because they did not understand it either, the journalists, that's why in this country on a daily level we talk more about Violencia(s) Machista(s) while GV is more for the official things, laws and it is the same, but it denotes an important evolution not only because the word is different but also young women and feminists want to pay attention to who is the one who respects the rules of machismo and commits violence, the men, that's why Violencia(s) Machista(s)... so it is the macho men who commit violence and I think that analyzing a little the terminology is very important because I believe that words construct thoughts.

[Spanish member of a national public administration
and policy expert interviewed in February 2020]

Since 2004, in the country, there is a clear legislation on Gender-Based Violence and since 1998, there are national plans and policies to eliminate Gender-Based Violence/Violence Against Women. As more than one interviewee has made clear, the State is responsible for marking the lines along which progress is to be made. Undoubtedly, laws and policies clearly depend on the government's agenda and political parties in power in specific moments:

> The 2004 law was the only law that was approved unanimously. This no longer happened with the Pacto de Estado in 2017 which is in line with the Istanbul Convention, and this is a clear difference in the vision of the parties. In 2004, only the judges were against VioGen, they had presented endless questions of unconstitutionality because they are the most conservative body in Spain, and they considered GV as a will of feminism to impose itself and that went against men, or that it simply GV did not exist ... recently instead, I'll give you an example, Vox (extreme right-wing party) did not even participate in the debates of the Pacto de Estado.

[Spanish policy expert and researcher interviewed in March 2020]

> Policy changes depend on the government at the time and the empathy and ideological connection to the issue.

[Spanish policy expert and member of a regional
organization, interviewed in March 2020]

In creating laws and policies and Government Responsiveness, the role of women's and feminist movements is also worth mentioning, with marches and protests, they hold the power to modify the priorities in the agenda-setting of the country (Bosch et al, 2006; García, 2016). The dialogue between movements and left-wing political parties, at most (Valiente, 2008), has created, especially during the Zapatero administration, a proficient level of GR. However, there are still things to do to address GBVAW, especially if we compare the current situation to the one that led to the VioGen Law of 2004 since the needs set out in a 2004 Law cannot be the same of a 2015 society; otherwise, this would mean that the society is not evolving. Moreover, one of the key issues is the lack of preventive measures in the VioGen and in other policies on the issue, as in this extract:

> Regarding the issue of prevention at the state level, it seems to me that the state focuses more on the after as if we had to accept that there are

Violencias Machistas. I personally like a phrase of the feminist movement "we do not want hospitals full of women or prisons full of men" because it is to assume that there will continue to be assaults, deaths, and femicides, and I think we must take a step towards society with preventive measures. Look, for me, in the Spanish institutional normative discourse, there is a prevalence of a punitive and penalist approach, and we need the implementation of a normative response that guarantees the human right to live a life free of violence because a democratic state has to guarantee human rights, if we understand that Violencias Machistas is not only a crime but a violation of human right, of women to live free of that violence, the response would be much more systemic, holistic, transversal, integrative.... it seems to me that we are trying to cover the sun with a finger - we must act a step earlier with prevention from a human rights approach.

[Spanish policy expert and researcher interviewed in March 2020]

There is also the way the Law adopts definitions and therefore measures to contrast the issue:

Spain is very afraid of revising the law, maybe because of if there is any kind of backtracking. So, I feel upset in that sense because I think we cannot say, well, we had a law that was a pioneer and think that we will be able to live off the top. Spain was and will always be a pioneer because it was the first one in 2004. So, I believe that one cannot aspire to simply live on the profits of that moment, right? And here I am a bit critical, that is, when the Istanbul Convention was ratified, I think they should have started to review the VioGen and see how it was, that is, whether or not it complied with the requirements of the Istanbul Convention and therefore all the forms of violence mentioned in it should be incorporated into the law itself. But, in order not to modify the law, an attempt has been made to make small patches at the level of the Penal Code, for instance, by including the crime of stalking, but without trying to make a comprehensive law, which would be more in line with the Istanbul Convention itself.

That reluctance to touch the law sometimes bothers me a little, together with the fear of questioning the concepts themselves, you know? I mean, the fact that Spain conceptualizes GV as violence within the couple is a bit reductionist. There is a small fear that the whole conceptual structure can be overturned; therefore, the country is opting for not touching what has already been achieved. But, in that sense, I am terribly upset.

[Spanish policy expert and member of a regional organization, interviewed in March 2020]

The criticisms, especially the narrow concept of GV, are restricted to the sphere of the partner or ex-partner. Another is the centrality of the Penal Code. For example, also for the outcomes of the laws on the topic, what has more weight is the Penal Code, which has more titles and articles. Another thing that happens is that protection is conditioned to the denunciation, with this being problematic. In other words, protection depends on the criminal complaint. That was one of the criticisms made at the time of the new Penal Code Reform. It is a criticism because it limits access, because let us see, the criminal field is complicated and extremely hard. It is exceedingly difficult, it has a lot of resistance, and then, with time, it has also been seen that women and girls also have a tremendous lack of credibility before the justice system. Then, in addition, there are situations in which it is said that it is possible to go, to have more options than the criminal complaint to make certain protection. Feminists have criticized the 2004 Law in general since there is little development of the social part because what it does is to collect reports of violence, opting for post-violence strategies. As we have said, it is a little bit a collection, but it does not develop it in a comprehensive manner and if it is called comprehensive assistance, it should be as such at the national level.

> [Spanish researcher, feminist activist and
> politician interviewed in March 2020]

However, more recently, laws and policies have proliferated and were improved thanks to the role of international and regional organizations.

European rules are mandatory in Spain, but it seems to me that the international level is a little more advanced than the national level. The Istanbul Convention and the GREVIO Committee, which has a significant role in the control of policies, see the actions of the states and the practices and report the status of the country at the international/UN level. I will give an example. In Spain, in 2014 the case of Ángela González Carreño - she filed 52 complaints because her husband had threatened to kill her daughter. Angela took it to court in Spain, and they did not give her the reason and she took it to the CEDAW committee, at the UN level, and it is the first case in Spain. From this sentence, it was necessary to change the law of 2004 to include with the reform of 2015 to the minors, it seems to me a very practical example of how the international field exercises control, examines the states and forces them via conviction to harmonize the rules ... and I also have hope in the GREVIO Committee because it forces the states to "present the duties" ... and also the role of the shadow reports of the NGOs and the organized communities of the feminist movements to make this control (requested by the UN) to have two versions instead of one (that of the state – that I like to call the world of Alice in Wonderland) and the shadow report, signed by more than 200 feminist organizations, that is to say they have an impact. It is like crossing the information and they force the states to give account of their actions and to become organized.

[Spanish policy expert and researcher interviewed in March 2020]

International documents are especially important, because if you sign them, you can demand the governments to comply with them... This is a little bit what happened with the PP, with Rajoy. Was the Pacto de Estado made with the PP because the popular party defended this? No, because there was an international commitment, there were the European institutions, and they saw that this was something absolutely demanded by Europe and supported by the whole socialist party. International documents are fundamental and especially useful and then every two years there is a gender report that EU MS must submit, and this is of crucial importance because this "to face Europe" is useful for governments to act on the issue.

[Spanish member of a national public administration
and policy expert interviewed in February 2020]

Finally, laws and national plans appear at a time of high dissemination of international documents on the subject, but they are also domestically driven (i.e., feminist and women's movements, left-wing and movements alliances, specific moments such as the 1997 murder of Ana Orantes). GV and VAW are often used as synonyms, but the approach of the former and that of machista(s) violencia(s) prevails. Transnational movements and women's groups, state feminism and women's movements have played a pivotal role in the development of laws and policies aimed at curbing GBVAW in Spain, and there have been important changes until recently: from policy to some cultural changes as one of the interviewed Spanish feminist activists asserted. These aspects are better explained with the following thematic lines that emerged from the interviews and the process tracing analysis carried out in this book:

Evolution of laws and policies in Spain

The laws and policies related to gender-based violence against women (GBVAW) in Spain have undergone significant changes since the transition to democracy in the late 1970s. The period from 1975 to 1978 marked a crucial phase in the establishment of democracy, and since then, there has been an acceleration in the development of laws and policies on this issue.

Definition of gender-based violence in Spain

The Spanish government's definition of gender-based violence, as outlined in the VioGen Organic Law of 2004 and subsequent dispositions in 2013 and 2015, recognizes it as a manifestation of inequality, subordination, and power imbalances between men and women. This definition highlights the importance of understanding gender violence as a structural problem rooted in gender discrimination and the lack of gender equality.

Preferred terminology: GV vs. Violencia(s) Machista(s)

In Spain, there is a preference for using the term "gender violence" (GV) in official documents and laws, as it encompasses violence in intimate partner relationships. However, there is also a growing recognition and use of the term "Violencia(s) Machista(s)" (macho/machista violence) to address a broader range of violence, including cultural, symbolic, and institutional forms. This term emphasizes that gender violence is predominantly perpetrated by men against women and underscores the comprehensive nature of the problem.

Influence of women's and feminist movements

Women's and feminist movements in Spain play a crucial role in shaping laws, policies, and the government's agenda. Through marches, protests, and advocacy efforts, these movements have successfully influenced the prioritization of gender-based violence and compelled left-wing political parties to address the issue. The collaboration between movements and political parties has resulted in a high level of government responsiveness.

Criticisms of existing laws and policies

Despite progress in addressing GBVAW, there are criticisms regarding the narrow definition of gender violence limited to intimate partner relationships. Some argue that the focus on the Penal Code and criminal complaints places undue emphasis on punitive measures rather than comprehensive prevention and protection strategies. There is a call for a more systemic and holistic approach to tackling GBVAW, incorporating preventive measures and a human rights perspective.

International and regional influence

International and regional organizations, such as the United Nations and the Council of Europe, have played a significant role in shaping laws and policies in Spain. The ratification of the Istanbul Convention and the oversight of the GREVIO Committee have prompted legislative reforms and harmonization of rules at the national level. Shadow reports from NGOs and feminist organizations have provided an additional avenue for scrutiny and accountability, pushing the government to address GBVAW more effectively.

Role of governments and political parties

The agenda and priorities regarding GBVAW largely depend on the government in power and its ideological alignment. The unanimity in passing the 2004 VioGen Law contrasted with the lack of consensus during the 2017 Pacto de Estado (State Pact), highlighting the differing visions of political parties on gender violence.

Need for comprehensive laws and policies

There is a need to update laws and policies to address the evolving challenges related to GBVAW. Critics argue that the current legal framework, including the VioGen Law, falls short in terms of comprehensive prevention, social development, and holistic assistance. The emphasis on the Penal Code and reliance on criminal complaints are seen as limitations that hinder access to protection. Finally, the interviews provide insights into various perspectives on GBVAW and the effectiveness of laws and policies in Spain. For instance, the recognition of GBVAW as a Structural Problem is not merely an issue of individual misfortune but a structural problem rooted in gender discrimination and patriarchy. It is seen as a mechanism employed to maintain control over women and preserve the status quo. The term "Violencia(s) Machista(s)" is favored by some interviewees for capturing the broader societal dimensions of the problem. Another key aspect is Government Responsiveness and Political Factors. Indeed, the interviewees highlight the importance of ideological alignment and empathy with the issue for effective government action. The unanimity in approving the 2004 VioGen Law and the subsequent changes in the political landscape demonstrate the influence of political factors. Last but not least, the need for Comprehensive and Preventive Approaches emerges from the interviews, meaning comprehensive approaches that go beyond the criminal aspect.

National and transnational movements of women on GBVAW

In Spain, the action of women's movements pushing for policies on violence is effective within institutional bodies (Corradi & Stöckl 2016). They are both active and very convinced in bringing their demands to the parliament for discussion.

> With democracy, many public policies for women began to be made and promoted by the public administration, and with the socialist governments

that have existed since the transition until now, there were feminist women in government and created many public policies for women and the feminist movement for some time was not as strong as before, did not have a strong presence in society ... in Spain it was the public administration that began public policies for women from the 80s (for instance in 1984 with the creation of the Women's Institute).

[Spanish member of a national public administration
and policy expert interviewed in February 2020]

The impact of international documents and transnational movements is also clear in Spain (Bustelo, 2016; Weldon & Htun, 2013; Montoya, 2013; Kantola, 2006) and has links with the action of national feminist movements:

Then in 2014 the Istanbul Convention came into force. Feminist movements and the Spanish one starts to use it as a claim as well. Not only that, but they also start to include it in their own demonstrations, as has also happened in 2015 during the demonstration of 25N when the PSOE asked for a Pacto de Estado contra la Violencia de Género.

[Spanish researcher, feminist activist and
politician interviewed in March 2020]

In Italy, the momentum of femocrats (Mazur, 2016) seems to be predominant compared to movements that seem to be in short supply, not so much in terms of existence (Weldon & Htun, 2013) but in terms of pressure on the government and dialogue with members of parliament (Valiente, 2005). It is worth noting how all the main laws on violence and women are passed because a female minister oversees them, only partly making use of the civic and moral conscience of women's movements.

Furthermore, the characteristics of feminist and women's movements are extremely diverse in the two countries, with this changing the way the two countries respond to GBVAW. In Spain, both the feminist and women's movements dialogued and interacted with the government. On the contrary, in Italy, the feminist movements decided not to associate with institutions and political power because they were looking for a cultural change and did not want to become "corrupted" in the political system. However, this choice hampered the evolution of any policies and laws to contrast GBVAW as a phenomenon, to protect victims of such acts, and to integrate men into the practices to counter the phenomenon. For this reason, in Italy, GR to GBVAW was the result of international pressure and advocacy, thus transnationally driven (Montoya, 2013), and of women in politics, especially those women who occupied a position of relevance in the Parliament. Whereas, in Spain, it was the double militancy of women in movements and leftist parties that resulted in comprehensive dispositions on the issue. For this reason, the path to VAW policy formation has been domestically driven (Montoya, 2013).

Moreover, GBVAW policies in Italy privilege "a predominantly emergency and security response" [Italian activist and researcher interviewed in June 2020], and this is a result of the way feminist movements (Della Porta, 2003) have acted in the country:

> Italian feminism has historically been more distrustful of the normative and institutional aspect because Italian feminism, perhaps rightly so, sought to do a little more work on the cultural, philosophical transformation of the imaginary; Spanish feminism, for example, had a more practical, concrete approach, linked to this dimension, and among other things the involvement of men in these campaigns is also more visible and more structured.
>
> [Italian activist and researcher interviewed in June 2020]

> Italian GBVAW policies and laws are conservative responses to emergency requests, always responses to such a request, if the result of international pressure, and always with non-preventive measures.
>
> [Italian activist and member of an international organization interviewed in April 2020]

Regarding movements, what has recently happened in Italy is:

> I see movements today that talk about women's freedom and are against violence but are walls asking the river not to flood us, not to send us back - a reaction to trying to bring everything back a little bit.
>
> [Italian researcher interviewed in May 2020]

> The relationship between national and local levels, for me that is the crux of the matter, you must get rid of this and everything else comes...in all of Italy there are no national feminist movements, we are a big country and even more anarchic.
>
> [Italian chairwoman of an association dealing with GBVAW and member of international organizations on the subject, interviewed in July 2020]

This is a substantial difference when considering that in Spain, the social fabric is more intricate, and there are both national and smaller feminist groups that accept the baton of the next challenges in the field of women's rights and the fight against GBVAW.

The analysis of the interviews highlights significant differences in the approaches and outcomes of women's movements and GBVAW policies in

Spain and Italy. In Spain, women's movements have been effective in pushing for policies on gender violence against women within institutional bodies. They actively bring their demands to parliament for discussion and have had a strong presence in society. The Spanish governments, particularly socialist governments, have played a role in creating public policies for women since the transition to democracy. Additionally, the impact of international documents and transnational movements, such as the Istanbul Convention, has influenced the actions of the Spanish feminist movement.

On the other hand, Italy has seen a predominant influence of femocrats and a relatively weaker presence of feminist movements. While feminist movements exist in Italy, they have chosen not to associate with institutions and political power, focusing instead on cultural change. This decision has hindered the evolution of policies and laws to combat GBVAW within the country. Instead, Italy's response to GBVAW has been driven by international pressure and advocacy, as well as the involvement of women in politics, particularly those in positions of relevance in the Parliament.

In terms of policy approaches, Italy's GBVAW policies lean towards emergency and security responses, with a conservative focus and limited preventive measures. This approach is reflective of the historical tendency of Italian feminism to prioritize cultural and philosophical transformation. In contrast, Spanish feminism has taken a more practical and concrete approach, emphasizing men's involvement and addressing the issue comprehensively.

The relationship between national and local levels is crucial in understanding the differences between the two countries. In Spain, the social fabric is more intricate, with both national and smaller feminist groups actively participating in the fight against GBVAW. In Italy, the absence of strong national feminist movements and the country's more anarchic nature make it challenging to coordinate efforts effectively.

In conclusion, these findings suggest that the formation of GBVAW policies in Spain has been domestically driven, with a strong presence of women's movements and leftist parties, while in Italy, it has been more transnationally driven, influenced by international pressure and the involvement of women in politics. The varying approaches and outcomes reflect the distinct cultural and political contexts of the two countries.

Chapter V

Comparing Italy and Spain on the level of GBVAW government responsiveness

Summary. The evolution of GBVAW/GV/VAW laws and policies in the two countries appears to be extremely different, although, in recent years, there has been a trend toward greater uniformity at the regional level (EU-CoE), which emphasizes the gender mainstreaming approach in both countries. This last chapter, before the conclusion, focuses on comparing laws and policies in the two countries in a fine-grained chronological analysis that makes sense of both countries' social changes. This chapter underlines that to have GR on GBVAW, the dialogue between the state, party politics, and movements has proved to be key in the two countries, in both the period under analysis as well as today.

Introduction

This chapter presents the two nation-states in a comparative perspective at both a regional and international level in order to highlight the differences between them and envision a broader EU framework of policies to contrast GBVAW.

Spain and Italy debate GBVAW policies differently, which is also clear in the definitions they use at the national level. Spain considers and mostly uses the expression GV by referring to the 2004 Organic Law on Gender Violence (in the Spanish normative system, a Law on fundamental rights and liberties), approved by unanimity of all the groups in Parliament and known as VioGen, and refers to VAW as occurring only between partners or former partners (in Spanish: parejas or ex-parejas). The general website of the Spanish Ministry for Equal Opportunities uses this definition: "Gender violence has been an invisible phenomenon for decades, being one of the clearest manifestations of inequality, subordination and power relations of men over women"[1] and the Law of 2004 specifies that GV includes all forms of physical and psychological violence including attacks on sexual freedom, threats, coercion or arbitrary deprivation of liberty[2] (Article 1.3, Organic Act 1/2004 of 28 December on Integrated Protection Measures Against Gender Violence). On the other hand, Italy refers to the definition used in the UN General Assembly resolution 48/104 of 1993, known as 'The Declaration on the Elimination of Violence Against Women (DEVAW),' and defines it as "any act of gender-based violence that results in, or is likely to result in, physical, sexual or psychological harm to women, including threats of such acts, coercion or arbitrary deprivation of liberty, whether occurring in public or in private life" (p. 3).

There are numerous reasons behind the differences in the definitions of the phenomenon and laws and policies in the two countries. For instance, in Spain, especially since the Zapatero government, from 2004, profound state feminism and grassroots feminist organizations led to domestically driven VAW reforms, while in Italy, feminist advocates had to interact with international networks to trigger government responsiveness, thus ensuing in transnationally driven reforms (Montoya, 2013, pp. 31-35). This is only one of the aspects that merits attention, the connection among different factors that eventually lead to the creation of specific laws, and later GBVAW policies, is key to consider.

Even though this specific chapter does not refer to the effectiveness of such progressive social policies, the comparison between these two Mediterranean countries might allow stakeholders and researchers to reflect on better practices to implement and ways to tackle broader social issues.

In conclusion, the latter concentrated on the comparison between the two nation-states and presented commonalities and differences in order to: a) propose a wider framework to address GBVAW at the EU level; b) show the different policy choices made at a national level by the two countries.

---

[1] In Spanish: '*La violencia de género se ha constituido como un fenómeno invisible durante décadas, siendo una de las manifestaciones más claras de la desigualdad, subordinación y de las relaciones de poder de los hombres sobre las mujeres.*' It also asserts that: '*La constatación de esta situación marcará un antes y un después en la consideración legal y social de los derechos y libertades de las mujeres*' ('The confirmation of the existence of this situation will mark a before and after in the legal and social consideration of the rights and freedoms of women'), therefore emphasizing the social and economic changes that this power relationship has on women's lives precisely because of the structure of society.

[2] In Spanish: '*La violencia de género a que se refiere la presente Ley comprende todo acto de violencia física y psicológica, incluidas las agresiones a la libertad sexual, las amenazas, las coacciones o la privación arbitraria de libertad.*'

Comparison and discussion of the results

Table 5.1 GBVAW actions by international organizations and governments (1993-2015)[3]

GBVAW ACTIONS BY INTERNATIONAL ORGANIZATIONS AND GOVERNMENTS (1993-2015)

YEAR	INTERNATIONAL ORGANIZATIONS (UN, COE, EU)	ITALY	SPAIN
1993-1998	(1993) UN-Declaration on the Elimination of VAW (1995) UN-Beijing World Conference on Women (1997) EU-Resolution campaign for zero tolerance of VAW; EU-Daphne program (still running)	**(1996) Law against sexual violence. Ministry of Equal Opportunities**	(1995) Law-Aid and assistance to victims of violent crimes and sexual freedom
1999-2004	(1999) UN-International Day for the Elimination of VAW (2000) UN-Resolution on elimination of crimes against women in the name of honour; EU-Charter of Fundamental Rights (2002) COE-Recommendation on the protection of Women against Violence (2003)EU-Resolution on violation of women's rights	(1998) Urban project 1 (2001) Law against violence in family relationships (2002) Urban Project 2	**(1998) First Action Plan against domestic violence** (2003) Law-protection order for domestic violence victims (2003) Law "Concrete measures regarding citizen security, domestic violence and social integration of foreigners" **(2004) Law VioGen, Equality Policies General Secretariat**
2005-2010	(2005) UN-Beijing+10 (2007) UN-Eliminating rape and other forms of sexual violence (2008) EU-Guidelines on violence and discrimination against women and girls (2009) EU-Parliament resolution on the elimination of VAW (2010) UN-Elimination of discrimination against women EU-Conclusions on the Eradication of VAW in the European Union EU-Women's Charter	(2006) Helpline 1522 **(2008) National action plan against sexual violence** (2009) Law against sexual violence and acts of persecution	(2005) Government Delegation for VAW (2007) Law for effective equality between women and men Helpline 016 National plan for awareness and prevention of gender violence (2008) Establishment of the Ministry of Equality (2010) Establishment of the Secretary of State for Equality

---

[3] Tab. 5.1. shows the most relevant actions dealing wih GBVAW from 1993 to 2015. The table is the author's own output.

		(2011) National action plan on women, peace and security	
2011-2015	(2011) COE-Istanbul Convention EU-Council Conclusions on the EU Pact for Gender Equality EU-Strategy for Equality between Women and Men (2015) UN-SDGs	**(2013) Law urgent provisions on security and fight against gender violence** **(2013) Ratification of the Istanbul CoE Convention** (2015) National plan against sexual violence	**(2013-2016) National Strategy for the Eradication of Violence against Women** (2013) Pacto de Estado contra la VG

A first comparative analysis of the laws and policies approved in the parliaments of the two Mediterranean countries provides a picture of similarities and/or differences between them. For instance, between 2011-2015, the significant impact of the Istanbul Conference on both the European Union and the individual countries is evident, demonstrating a huge influence of the international and regional organizations on the approval of GBVAW/VAW/GV laws and policies in Italy and Spain, despite the relatively few clear-cut differences. Italy could not have proposed such a comprehensive Law in 2013 and a national plan in 2015 if it were not to receive the 2011 Istanbul Convention: both the national governments and majority parties in Parliament were not particularly attentive to the issue, the same thing with the presence of feminist or women's movements interested in the phenomenon: they will increase in number and consistency after 2015, as a reaction to the SDGs and to the #metoo movement (Parmegiani & Prevedello, 2019; Donato, 2020). In comparison, Spain had and still has both strong state feminism and women's and feminist movements that struggle to get laws and policies approved (Bustelo, 2016; Threlfall et al., 2005). Moreover, from 2003 to 2015,[4] the right-wing parties in the Parliament have not stopped their fight against GBVAW, proving that the issue is a priority in the country's political agenda and not an ideological issue.

Chronologically, Italy started to deal with violence in 1996, with the Law that establishes the rules against sexual violence (Lagostena Bassi et al., 1997). The document approved in the national territory is, however, exempt from direct references to 'subjects.' In the following years, this characteristic turns out to

---

[4] The situation has slightly changed since 2015, with the emergence of an extreme right-wing party (VOX), despite the national left-wing government coalition (PSOE-Podemos) continues the implementation of the 2017 State Pact and the fight against Violencia(s) Machista(s). For more information see: https://violenciagenero.igualdad.gob.es/instituciones/delegacionGobierno/home.htm

be a peculiarity of the Italian Laws on the issue. The only body that started to deal with women as a specific sector of society is the Department for equal opportunities, created in 1996. Moreover, violence only stopped being considered purely physical in 2013. The flexibility with which Italy handles this social problem is relevant, with there being no clear reference to gender-based violence or violence against women.

The opposite is the case in Spain. The law that defines the attention of Spanish society and created an important watershed in the field of gender-based violence is the 2004 Organic Law on comprehensive protection measures against gender-based violence. The creation of a specific institute for women and the strong will to defeat and prevent violence are, for Spain, of focal importance for clear planning of national instruments to hinder the violent path of men toward women. In addition, Spain has its own definition of violence, unlike Italy, which uses the cornerstones of the 1993 UN resolution. Moreover, the clear preponderance of one theoretical approach over the other is visible in Spain. The preference is for GV, although in some official texts, the two expressions are used as synonymous, Law and policymakers, as well as civil society, are aware of the differences and are also using a new way to refer to it: Violencia(s) Machista(s). Furthermore, since 2003 Spain has preferred a gender mainstreaming approach, with the abolishment of gender discrimination (Bodelón, 2013). On the other hand, Italy moves between gender invisibility, as in the case of the 1996 Law and women's only (Walby et al., 2017; Corradi & Donato, 2019), with a significant lack of national contextualization since its GBVAW laws and policies are the results of international soft power and, thus transnationally driven (Montoya, 2013), but remain relatively issue-oriented and conservative until 2013 when they are approved and framed in the national scenario exclusively by the right-wing political parties.

Moreover, while in Spain, the issue of VAW was already present in the public sphere at the end of the Francoist dictatorship, with the creation of the Institute for Women in 1983 (in Italy, the Ministry of equal opportunities was created in 1996 as part of a new political environment in the country and as a possible outcome of Law 66/1996) and with the approval of a Law on the subject in 1989 – developing the first national plan to combat VAW in 1998 and generating the Organic Law 1/2004, on 28 December called 'Medidas de Protección Integral contra la Violencia de Género' [Organic Law on integrated protective measures against gender-based violence], also known as VioGen. In Spain, the presence of feminist movements and femocrats has proved to be of pivotal importance in order to institutionalize claims at the national level (Valiente, 2005; Lombardo & Léon, 2014). This is a dynamic that is missing in the Italian territory, despite there being evident space for the practice of regional diffusion at the EU level and considering the high autonomy of feminist and women's movements in the country (Cavarero & Rastaino, 2002; Rossi-Doria, 2005; Htun & Weldon, 2012; Corradi & Bandelli, 2018).

Finally, in Spain, a preponderant gender mainstreaming, the constant dialogue between feminist movements, women's movements, political parties, and national administrations and bodies, have allowed since 2003 the simplest and most direct institutionalization of demands concerning gender equality and the fight against GBVAW. On the other hand, in Italy, gender as a policy component is little considered, with there being a debate on equal opportunities and a ministry specialized in this aspect more than in contrast to GBVAW. The gender mainstreaming approach and comprehensive policy strategies on GBVAW: comprising preventive more than just post-violence ones, training for experts and male integration in the debate, abandoning the often-misleading women's only approach, have only recently emerged with the international pressure of the CoE and UN, the ratification of the Istanbul Convention and the willingness to abide by some of the international treaties and challenges, as the one of the SDGs. However, the laws on the matter continue to be single-issue, emergency, and security-oriented ones. The lack of a specific court for this kind of violence and a law regulating the entirety of this matter shows hostility towards the phenomenon and the understanding that its structural and cultural roots are so deep that only a very precise, detailed, punitive, but also re-educational structure can prevent this phenomenon from remaining an unsolvable social problem. In Spain, there is an integral law, but it does not regulate all forms of gender-based violence, as already discussed in the previous paragraphs. However, this law provides specific measures that allow for a life free from violence to all those who decide to report or turn to the specific services distributed throughout the national territory, despite the autonomic characteristic of the Spanish territory. In addition, as a counter-narrative to "VioGen it's enough," in 2017, the government approved the Pact of State that renews and expands the concept of Gender-Based Violence Against Women, incorporates the latest demands of the feminist and women's movements, as well as the dictates of the international bodies (for example GREVIO and CEDAW).

Driving change: a comparative analysis of GBVAW policies in Spain and Italy

This book has delved into the evolution of Gender-Based Violence Against Women (GBVAW) laws and policies in Spain and Italy, highlighting the significant differences between the two countries. While recent years have shown a trend towards greater uniformity at the regional level, with a focus on gender mainstreaming within the EU-CoE framework, the factors that influenced the reception and integration of international and regional documents into national laws and policies varied in each country.

Key factors shaping the differing approaches to GBVAW policy creation include the interests and positions of political parties in power, the level of dialogue between political entities and feminist movements, the influence of EU presidency terms held by Italy and Spain, and the presence or absence of femocrats and state feminism. Additionally, the level of adherence to EU directives and resolutions as a priority for the state and government played a crucial role.

In detail, after the presentation on the evolution of GBVAW laws and policies and their analysis in the two countries, it is possible to claim that in Spain and Italy, the factors that produced a different reception of the international and regional documents within national laws and systems of policies were:

1. The interest the parties in power and their position had in relation to the issue.

2. The dialogue or lack of dialogue between the latter and both feminist and women's movements.

3. The role of the presidencies that Italy and Spain held at the EU level.

4. The importance of femocrats and state feminism in translating the requests of the movements and the civil society (Spain) or the complete absence of it (Italy).

5. The respect of the EU directives and resolutions on the matter as a state and a government priority (RQs).

Therefore, over the period 1993-2015, Spain coupled transnational advocacy, the respect of international documents, and its integration into the national normative system with the requests of the feminist movements, thus fostering the level of GR in the country, with a peak during the Zapatero government (2004-2011) but maintaining the trend also during the PP conservative rule of Mariano Rajoy, thus establishing the crucial importance of the topic in the agenda-setting of the country.

In Italy, the level of GR was mostly the result of the reception of international documents, especially of the CoE and the EU (because they often imply binding measures) in the national Italian system of laws and policies. However, the role of transnational advocacy coupled with the emergency approach to the matter that characterizes Italy. The laws and policies were either the result of dramatic events and the will to answer specifically to physical and sexual violence or the transposition of resolutions, reports, directives, and conventions in the Italian normative system and were influenced by the possibilities of public subventions (especially from the EU, as the Resolutions related to the Daphne programs or Urban Projects) in order to be approved (RQ3).

In conclusion, to have GR on GBVAW, the dialogue between the state, party politics, and movements has proved to be key. At the same time, the role of international and regional organizations in framing and proposing strategies to address GBVAW is fundamental for the creation of laws and policies, especially in those countries, such as Italy, where social movements, in this case, feminist movements, have difficulty confronting the government in power (for ideological reasons, positions or conservative vs. progressive systems) and the institutions and encounter obstacles in reaching protection and preventive measures to counter GBVAW nationally.

Finally, the EU framework is – without a doubt – still lacking the implementation step in practice, but it is already influencing the way governments and politics look at GBVAW in both countries: a social issue that has to be wiped out once and for all with a comprehensive structural, and cultural, transformation, by producing an acceleration in the national more conservative policy practices of Italy which from 1996 to 2015 also experienced the lack of both social and feminist fabric.

Unveiling contrasting responses: GBVAW policies in times of crisis

Gender-Based Violence Against Women is an issue that can become worse in times of crisis. Actions taken by numerous nations during the 2020 pandemic have demonstrated that institutions must take caution in how they respond to such recurrent social issues in times of crisis.

The responses from the Spanish and Italian governments were significantly different. A situation that occurred even though both governments supported the recommendations and call to action issued by United Nations Secretary-General António Guterres to combat "the horrifying global surge in domestic violence."[5] This led to extensive institutional knowledge, active engagement in movements, and involvement of the entire civil society in Spain, all of which aided in the creation of procedures and regulations to deal with GBVAW throughout the pandemic.

Spain developed a number of additional alternative measures to its customary ones since the beginning of March, including the proclamation of the state of emergency on March 13, and its coming into effect on March 14. The Spanish Ministry of Equality claimed that calls to the 016 helpline services rose as the pandemic lockdown in March 2020 took effect. Additionally, the Spanish government decided to declare all services involved in the comprehensive

---

[5] See un.org for more information about the statement by UN Secretary-General António Guterres.

protection of victims of gender-based violence, such as anti-violence centers,[6] and all locations that provide essential security with the Royal Decree 12/2020 of March 31 (Ruiz-Pérez & Pastor-Moreno, 2020), such as housing, legal advice, and emotional support. As part of its response to the government delegation against gender-based violence, Spain also made available an easy-to-read guide for women[7] seeking aid as well as an updated map of the services provided by autonomous communities and towns. During the COVID-19 pandemic, the government established an emergency plan for addressing gender-based violence and enacted a particular ordinance. It stated that autonomous communities may use State Pact funds that were not used in 2019 to combat GBVAW in addition to identifying vital services for GBVAW victims. The Spanish government's quick response was intense from the start of the pandemic and reflected the institutional level and civil society's existing good cooperation and communication. Since the emergency lockdown began, a specialized program was established to address incidents of violence while confined. The Official Pharmacists Association promoted the Mascarilla 19 program, which was started in the Canary Islands, far away from the peninsula. It rapidly extended across the entirety of the Spanish national territory as part of the nation's efforts to halt the coronavirus curve without triggering GV cases. It worked in this way: pharmacies served as a resource where people may turn for assistance and report cases. In a very discreet manner, the pharmacist also notifies the police and the prosecution's special department dealing with gender violence.

Conversely, Italy's level of engagement was not as profound as Spain's. The government supported the first model used in Spain, primarily because of a campaign with the hashtag #liberapuoi[8], and the action taken by Spain, Mascarilla 19, was recognized as a credible effort to address GBVAW. However, it resulted in several practices and intentions without any concrete safeguards for women who suffered from violence.

Spain approved the Royal Decree 12/2020 and determined to regard as essential all services that protect and aid victims of gender-based violence, whereas Italy neither approved a specific contingency plan nor permitted local

---

[6] Real Decreto-ley 12/2020 of urgent measures to protect and assist victims of gender-based violence, of March 31. Available at: https://www.boe.es/boe/dias/2020/04/01/pdfs/BOE-A-2020-4209.pdf.

[7] For more information see this website: https://violenciagenero.igualdad.gob.es/informacion Util/covid19/home.htm

[8] For more information see this website: https://www.governo.it/it/media/campagna-di-comunicazione-contro-la-violenza-sulle-donne-2021-libera-puoi/18622.

services, such as ensuring a direct protocol to follow at pharmacies, to be provided in the country.

Once again, this brief picture of the government responsiveness adopted by the two countries ascertains that since 2004, the government in Spain has expanded its services to address gender-based violence in all circumstances, and this included emergency times such as the COVID-19 pandemic and the lockdown. More specifically, in Spain, throughout the pandemic, the institutions' services and attention remained consistent and improved. Among these, there was the ATENPRO telephone service for GV victims' protection and attention, a telematic monitoring system to manage restraining orders overseen by the Ministry of the Interior's Secretariat of State for Security. Italy, on the contrary, did not act to protect and prevent GBVAW occurrences and resorted to simply informing the citizens.

Conclusions

This book has shed light on the importance of international and regional organizations in shaping the agenda on women's issues. It has emphasized the significance of explicit national legislation in addressing various forms of Gender-Based Violence Against Women (GBVAW) and ensuring that violence is not ignored or unpunished. As in Montoya (2013, p.7), once explicit legislation exists, there is "less room for interpretation that may allow violence to be ignored or go unpunished."

By comparing the cases of Italy and Spain from 1993 to 2015, the book has revealed that the differences in the evolution of laws and policies can be attributed to the dissimilar reception of international documents in the two countries, as well as the action of transnational and local organizations and movements in fostering national action. Moreover, historical processes and national changes in politics influenced the agenda-setting of the two countries, with any eventual alterations in the development of policies on GBVAW – considered as either a priority or not – being no exception. Left-wing-oriented parties in the national government in specific periods fostered GR on GBVAW in Italy and Spain. The dialogue between the civil society and the institutional level has proved to be of paramount importance in having GBVAW government responsiveness and policymaking.

The main goal of this book has been to contribute to the understanding and the design of laws and policies concerning GBVAW in the specific cases of Italy and Spain, to frame the differences in two countries that are often considered as similar, but that in this specific section of social progressive policies differ enormously.

One of the main things that has emerged from this book, and is therefore worth highlighting, is how in Italy, precisely because of the lack of dialogue between the institutions and the civil society, those laws and policy measures that are crucial to combat Gender-Based Violence Against Women are less comprehensive and generally do not integrate women's and feminist requests coming from society. They are predominately the result of international documents in the sense that national laws and policies appear only when international and/or regional binding documents call for the country to act against GBVAW. On the contrary, international laws and policies on GBVAW in Spain are also expressions of the requests of feminist and women's movements and organizations. They are less inducted by the adoption of international and regional documents precisely because most of the calls and demands of the international and regional organizations and documents are already integrated into the national system of laws and policies.

This book has also highlighted one specific aspect: regions play their role in legislating and influencing single nation-states to implement policy measures to counter GBVAW. For this reason, this book suggests that it is possible to reach a broader EU framework of policies on GBVAW, starting by analyzing and comparing case studies.

I will now try to discuss this book's RQs and later discuss the general outcomes of the book, limits of the same, and future research perspectives:

Table 5.1 provides a summary of actions taken by international organizations and governments regarding Gender-Based Violence Against Women (GBVAW) between 1993 and 2015. These actions are essential for addressing the research questions posed in this book.

Research Question 1 seeks to identify the most significant international documents on GBVAW from 1993 to 2015, focusing on their importance for individual EU nation-states such as Italy and Spain. Several key documents produced by the United Nations (UN), Council of Europe (CoE), and European Union (EU) stand out:

1. DEVAW UN Resolution of 1993. (It framed the issue of GBVAW, and it is still the main definition used in many states, as well as the only definition Italy adopts with reference to VAW. The most prevalent approach on the issue in Italy is still VAW, and this reflects the international organization's moral suasion and transferable narrative on the issue of GBVAW. The Resolution is also crucially significant because it considers acts and threats of violence, thus going beyond mere physical violence and proofs of abuse, and it also considers violence to be a public issue, not to be relegated to a private matter (it has often been considered as a couple's issue). This has been significant in the later development of documents and policies on GBVAW).

2. UN-Beijing World Conference on Women in 1995 was also important (It asserts that VAW is the result of unequal and historical power relations between men and women, that violence is a form of discrimination that is usually directed at women, and that it violates and nullifies human rights).

3. EU- Resolution campaign for zero tolerance of VAW and EU Daphne program in 1997 (It envisaged the creation of regional measures to raise awareness and creative, practical outcomes to contrast GBVAW).

4. The creation of UN-International Day for the Elimination of VAW in 1999 (It is a clear international declaration of intents shared by all the

MSs, asserting that women should not fear to live a life free from violence).

5.   UN Resolution on the elimination of crimes against women in the name of honor in 2000 (It acts to condemn national and specific contexts that still see women as an inferior part of society and therefore accept the violations of women's rights in the name of honor).

6.   CoE Recommendation on the Protection of Women against Violence in 2002 (It centers on active educational training, public awareness campaigns, and men's role in ending violence. It also fosters the creation of a body controlling the implementation of measures to combat violence regionally, as well as the advancement of the role of media and modern technologies in avoiding the promotion of a "stereotyped image of men and women.").

7.   EU Parliament resolution on the elimination of VAW in 2009 (It is momentously relevant since operative clause number 25 proposes "a view to encouraging a Europewide exchange of good practice," as a way to guarantee the right to assistance and support for all the victims of violence); together with the EU Women's Charter and the conclusions on the eradication of VAW in the EU in 2010;

8.   CoE Istanbul Convention, EU Strategy for Equality between Women and Men in 2011 (It creates the 4 Ps approach: protection, prevention, and persecution, respectively, of victims, of VAW and offenders, and integrated policies. It also establishes the creation of the Group of Experts on Action against Violence against Women and Domestic Violence).

9.   UN SGS in 2015 set up measures to contrast GBVAW/VAW (It establishes goals and targets to be achieved by 2030, like target 16.1, which aims to: 'Significantly reduce all forms of violence and related death rates everywhere' and Target 16.3 that focuses on the promotion of 'the rule of law at the national and international levels and ensure equal access to justice for all,' and SDG 5 (5.2) that includes a target to eliminate all forms of violence against women and girls).

In these documents and declarations of the UN, CoE, and EU, the narratives and categories of reference to the phenomenon of GBVAW varied a lot in the period analyzed, with them having an influence on the way Spain and Italy reacted and responded, with reference to the first step of policymaking, to violence as perpetrated against one specific part of the society. From a purely private issue, GBVAW slowly started to be seen as a problem that undermines equality between men and women, and gender mainstreaming approaches were later added, therefore considering women not only as vulnerable subjects and victims but also as subjects endowed with agency.

Research Question 2 explores the factors contributing to the different reception of international and regional documents within the national laws and policies of Spain and Italy. The book highlights several variables that shaped the response in each country, including: Political parties in power and their prioritization of GBVAW interventions and policies; media focus and attention on GBVAW; the involvement of women's and feminist movements in dialogue with institutions and governments; the representation of these movements within the political sphere, influencing policymaking; and the role of regional binding measures that obliged adherence to EU recommendations and the Istanbul Convention.

Indeed, following a chronological order of the events but also comparing different time periods, this book shows how the presence of specific political parties in power and their agenda-oriented GBVAW interventions and priorities, or the lack of interest towards them; the evolution of international declarations of intents and the moral suasion of the international bodies influenced laws and policies differently in the two countries: a push for Italian laws and policies and an additional value, an accelerator to the already existing measures to counter GBVAW in Spain. However, regional binding measures proved to be more relevant than international documents since they obliged the two countries to abide by the principles of EU recommendations, decisions, and other measures. This is evident with the creation of the Daphne programme, the respect of the EU Women's Charter, the signing and implementation of the Istanbul Convention, and specific questions that were posed to the EU bodies and that directed the attention to the phenomenon, as with the written question of Christine Oddy to the Commission in 1996, thus leading to transnational advocacy that fostered the actions of women's and feminist movements and organizations locally.

Women's and feminist movements also played a role of paramount importance in influencing laws and policies, regimes, settings, and measures on GBVAW. This has also proved to be different in the sense that the dialogue or lack of dialogue between movements and institutions led to policymaking on GBVAW. Specifically, women's and feminist movements in Spain were strong but not autonomous. Since the beginning of the democratic period, after the end of the Francoist dictatorship, they led to rapid GBVAW policy change, looking for a dialogue with governments and parties in politics. They also become part of governments, especially within the context of the PSOE and Podemos parties. Thus creating an awareness on GBVAW and producing GR on the issue. In Italy, on the contrary, women's movements have always been proudly autonomous and very disinterested in triggering government action. The lack of femocrats in politics and women's policy agency in disciplining and prioritizing measures and actions to contrast GBVAW was also evident in Italy and resulted from the lack of interaction and dialogue between the government, institutions, as well as any movements and organizations.

For Research Question 3, which focuses on the differential responses of Italy and Spain to GBVAW, particularly in terms of government responsiveness, the following scheme highlights the key legislative and policy measures taken by each country since 1993:

In Italy:

1. Law against sexual violence and the establishment of the Ministry of equal opportunities in 1996 (It represents a watershed in the understanding and punishment of sexual offenses and violence committed against women: it abolishes crimes against morality and identifies acts of sexual violence as acts to be legally punished since they are acts against the person).

2. Urban project in 1998 (It provides for specific measures in some Italian cities to respond to post-violence events against women).

3. Law against violence in family relationships in 2001 (It introduces protection orders as part of the Penal Code and the removal of violent men from the family home).

4. Urban Project 2 in 2002 (Similar to the first period of the Project, but also includes men in the debate and interviews perpetrators).

5. The creation and funding of a national helpline (1522) in 2006.

6. National action plan against sexual violence in 2008 (It contains the allocation of supporting measures to victims of sexual and GV, as stated in the text of the official National Gazette and comes from the reception and pressure of EU and CoE recommendations).

7. Law against sexual violence and acts of persecution in 2009 (It introduces a number of aggravating factors to the crimes of sexual violence and considers the crime of stalking acts of persecution).

8. National action plan on women, peace, and security in 2011 (It promises to develop information campaigns and training courses for all the relevant stakeholders on the issue of VAW and to implement an ad-hoc funded strategy).

9. Law on urgent provisions on security and fight against gender violence and the ratification of the Istanbul CoE Convention in 2013 (It represents the moment when Italy begins to address, more comprehensively and within official documents, the concept of gender. With this Convention, once integrated into the national legislative framework, GV, GBVAW,

and MVAW, have become new formulations of the phenomenon that are used in national laws and policies and have – since then – characterized Italian national debates on the matter).

10. National plan against sexual violence in 2015 (It provides for a system of monitoring and evaluation of good practices of multi-level governance, from local to national and shared within Europe).

In Spain:

1. Law-Aid and assistance to victims of violent crimes and sexual freedom in 1995 (It regulates the access to a system of public aid for the direct and indirect victims of violent crimes, despite only comprising: death, serious body injury, or considerable damage to physical or mental health).

2. First action plan against domestic violence in 1998 (It expands the measures aimed at countering the phenomenon of violence, and it includes preventive measures, education, and training; it also represents the beginning of the discussions that will lead to the organic law on GV).

3. Law protection order for domestic violence victims and law on concrete measures regarding citizen security, domestic violence, and social integration of foreigners in 2003.

4. Law VioGen and the establishment of the Equality Policies General Secretariat in 2004 (VioGen introduces a special Court of Violence against Women and the Prosecutor's Office against Violence against Women. VioGen is an integral law that specifically legislates on this matter, unprecedented in European contexts and first in the country's history).

5. The establishment of the government delegation for VAW (*contra la Violencia sobre la Mujer*) in 2005.

6. Law for effective equality between women and men; helpline and national plan for the awareness and prevention of gender violence in 2007 (The National Plan establishes the creation of specific training services for professionals in sectors ranging from justice, health, security services, and labor and social assistance, programs that propose measures that respect the principles of gender equality in schools (starting from elementary school), and finally, the creation of reintegration services for victims, as well as for the aggressors);

7. The establishment of the Ministry of Equality in 2008 and the Secretary of State for Equality in 2010.

8. The national pact against GV and the National strategy for the eradication of VAW in 2013-2016 (This strategy aims at both GV against multiple subjects and VAW, including new forms of physical violence such as trafficking and genital mutilation and online forms of GV).

Hence, the policy responses and laws addressing GBVAW in Italy and Spain were influenced by various intervening variables within their socio-political contexts. These factors encompassed the priorities of political parties in power, the media's focus, the role of feminist movements and women's agencies in dialogue with institutions and governments, as well as their involvement in party politics, leading to actions related to state feminism and women's policy agencies.

In Spain, left-wing political parties, particularly socialist parties, played a specific role in responding to the demands of Spanish society regarding GBVAW. They prioritized these issues and took active measures to address them. On the other hand, in Italy, left-wing parties did not give priority to GBVAW concerns. Instead, their focus was more on superficial attempts at promoting gender equality and parity, such as implementing "quotas for women" and similar initiatives. As a result, they failed to adequately incorporate women's voices and rights into national actions and the overall scenario.

The divergence in government responsiveness to GBVAW can be attributed to the differing influences on policy formulation in the two countries. In Spain, international and regional documents and declarations served as catalysts, augmenting existing laws and policies that emerged from the demands and needs of the movements and civil society. In contrast, Italy lacked substantial interaction and dialogue with women's movements and feminist realities. As a consequence, international and regional conventions and documents became launching pads for legislative efforts in Italy. However, these measures were less comprehensive and contextually nuanced, primarily because they were less attentive to the actual requests of civil society.

In conclusion, the research carried out in this book confronts some important aspects that literature until now has not addressed. It has examined how international and regional documents have produced a different narrative on the phenomenon: switching from battered women and victimization of women to concepts like agency, empowerment, and gender mainstreaming, to the influence they have or do not produce on national systems of laws and policies, the role of moral suasion concerning GV/VAW/GBVAW in the international scenario, together with transnational advocacy, women's and feminist organizations and movements, and the importance of GR as a constant trend in order not only to fight GBVAW but to prevent its occurrences globally. This book has provided a broad overview of the evolution of international and regional documents on GBVAW that has been carried out with different qualitative methods and, mostly thanks to process tracing, in-depth interviews, and qualitative text analysis; it has compared two cases that current literature often considers as similar.

While this study provides a comprehensive overview of the evolution of international and regional documents on GBVAW, it acknowledges certain limitations. One limitation is the exclusive focus on gender violence perpetrated against women, without delving into the experiences of other gender-related violence or violence resulting from other social discriminations. This choice is not ideological but rather aims to address the specific vulnerability of women who are still, and unfortunately, victims of violence. Another limitation of the investigation regards the analysis and comparison of only two case studies in contraposition to a broad range of comparative experiences or a panel of countries as in other studies (Htun & Weldon, 2012; Montoya, 2013; Corradi & Stöckl, 2016). This choice was the result of the acknowledgment that there is a gap in the current literature on the comparative public and socially progressive policies activities with an echo to GBVAW that specifically concerns the two Mediterranean states. The comparison aimed to show the differences and similarities between the two countries while also proposing the adoption of a wider, shared international framework of laws, policies, and best practices to address the issue of male violence perpetrated against women. An EU framework is considered a first step towards tackling GBVAW, despite it not being considered as exhaustive and global as a UN framework, which involves 193 countries and has a global voice. Finally, another limitation of the book refers to the methodological choice of multi-methods with a prevalence of qualitative approaches compared to quantitative. This decision lies in the willingness to portray new ways of making sense of the policy responses to GBVAW. It is my personal and scientific belief that it is crucial to start questioning the way we frame the problem of GBVAW by focusing on the theoretical approaches – explicitly and implicitly mentioned – by single nation-states in order to propose actual solutions to GBVAW to compare how governments respond to the request of the movements and the civil society, along with listening to experts point of views, thanks to in-depth interviews.

Future research should investigate the possibilities of establishing and proposing a global framework of laws, policies, and practices to address and abide by the same principles of human rights as women's rights, to account for gender mainstreaming approaches in policymaking and to question gender invisibility when aiming to contrast GBVAW. This could be carried out thanks to other studies on comparative cases. Data should also be collected in a way that is comparable at both the EU and International levels to share best practices and improve women's health and empowerment, but also to assure that women's lives are always free from violence.

Appendices

Appendix 1: Outline of the interview (in Italian)

Area d'indagine	Categorie di riferimento	Domande
Conoscenza ed esperienza diretta del fenomeno	Violenza di genere Violenza contro le donne Altro?	Mi piacerebbe sapere qualcosa in più su di lei, come si è avvicinata al fenomeno delle violenza di genere/ contro le donne? Perché?
	Uguaglianza di genere	Secondo lei, esiste una connessione, un vincolo tra uguaglianza di genere e violenza di genere? In caso affermativo, in che termini? Ad esempio: esistono casi di donne che lottano per l'uguaglianza ma che, in ogni caso, sono state vittime di violenza?
Partecipazione	Leggi, politiche Ricerca Attivismo	Come e per quanto tempo ha partecipato ad attività legate a questo tema? 1. Leggi- politiche 2. Interesse accademico- ricerca
	GBVAW- aspetti trattati	Temi trattati Su quale aspetto si è specializzata/o in tema di donne e violenza e perché?
Politiche GBVAW	Attori: Istituzioni, movimenti, persone	Quali sono gli attori che giocano un ruolo importante e che influiscono sul grado di *responsiveness* dei governi alla GBVAW?
	Istituzioni, movimenti, persone Natura e rilevanza del vincolo.	Esiste un vincolo tra le istituzioni e i movimenti? Quanto importante è il vincolo che esiste tra le istituzioni e i movimenti su questo tema? Come si crea il vincolo? Quali sono gli ostacoli più ovvi? Come funziona questa connessione nel tempo? Le persone fanno la differenza? Perché? Mi darebbe alcuni esempi nella storia recente del paese che vanno in questa direzione?

Importanza dei livelli: internazionale, regionale (UE, COE), nazionale	Governo-livello nazionale	Il governo al potere/ i cambi di governo (quello che accade su base nazionale) influiscono sulle politiche di GBVAW? Come? Esempi nella storia recente del paese
	Livello regionale e internazionale	Che impatto/influenza hanno l'Unione Europea e le altre entità internazionali sul tema delle leggi e politiche sulla GBVAW? Esiste un quadro comune oppure predomina il livello nazionale?
	Italia	A livello italiano, e basato sulla sua esperienza personale, quali sono le azioni positive che il paese ha messo in atto sul tema della GBVAW negli ultimi 20-25 anni? Quali sono le sfide attuali e cosa resta da fare in tema di GBVAW?

Appendix 2: Outline of the interview (in Spanish)

Área de investigación	Categorías de referencia	Preguntas
Conocimiento y experiencia directa del fenómeno	Violencia de género Violencia contra las mujeres ¿Otros?	Me gustaría saber más sobre su experiencia personal, ¿Cómo se acercó al fenómeno de la violencia de género y contra las mujeres? ¿Por qué?
	Igualdad de género	En su opinión, ¿existe una conexión, un vínculo entre la igualdad de género y la violencia de género? Si es así, ¿en qué términos? Por ejemplo: ¿hay casos de mujeres que luchan por la igualdad pero que, en cualquier caso, han sido víctimas de violencia de género?
Participación	Leyes, políticas Investigación Activismo	¿Cómo y durante cuánto tiempo ha participado en actividades relacionadas con este tema? 1. Leyes - políticas 2. Interés académico - investigación
	GBVAW- aspectos de interés	Temas tratados ¿En qué aspecto de la GBVAW se ha especializado y por qué?
Políticas GBVAW	Actores implicados: instituciones, movimientos, personas	¿Cuáles actores desempeñan un papel importante e influyen en el grado de respuesta de los gobiernos a la GBVAW?
	Instituciones, movimientos, personas El carácter del vínculo y la relevancia respectiva.	¿Existe un vínculo entre las instituciones y los movimientos? ¿Qué importancia tiene el vínculo entre las instituciones y los movimientos en este tema? ¿Cómo se crea el enlace? ¿Cuáles son los obstáculos más evidentes? ¿Cómo funciona esta conexión a lo largo del tiempo? ¿Las personas marcan la diferencia? ¿Por qué? ¿Podría darme algunos ejemplos en la historia reciente del país que vayan en esta dirección?
Importancia de los niveles: internacional, regional (UE, COE), nacional	Nivel gubernamental-nacional	¿Afectan el gobierno de turno y los cambios de gobierno (lo que ocurre a nivel nacional) a las políticas de violencia contra la mujer?

		¿Cómo? Ejemplos en la historia reciente del país
	Nivel regional e internacional	¿Qué impacto/influencia tienen la UE y otras entidades internacionales en la cuestión de las leyes y políticas sobre la GBVAW? ¿Existe un marco común o predomina el nivel nacional?
	Italia	A nivel español , y basándose en su experiencia personal, ¿cuáles son las acciones positivas que el país ha implementado en el tema de la GBVAW en los últimos 20-25 años? ¿Cuáles son los retos actuales en materia de GBVAW?

Bibliography

Adler, J. S. (2003). "We've Got a Right to Fight; We're Married": Domestic Homicide in Chicago, 1875–1920. *Journal of Interdisciplinary History, 34*(2), 27-48. https://doi.org/10.1162/002219503322645448

Aksan, N., Kısac, B., Aydın, M., & Demirbuken, S. (2009). Symbolic interaction theory. *Procedia-Social and Behavioral Sciences, 1*(1), 902-904. https://doi.org/10.1016/j.sbspro.2009.01.160

Anguera, M. T., Portell, M., Chacón-Moscoso, S., & Sanduvete-Chaves, S. (2018). Indirect observation in everyday contexts: concepts and methodological guidelines within a mixed methods framework. *Front. Psychol, 9*(13). https://doi.org/10.3389/fpsyg.2018.00013

Artazcoz, L., Cortés, I., Puig-Barrachina, V., Benavides, F.G. Escribà-Aguir, V., & Borrell, C. (2013). Combining employment and family in Europe: the role of family policies in health. *European Journal of Public Health, 24*(4), 649-655. https://doi.org/10.1093/eurpub/ckt170

Bacchi, C. (2012). Why study problematizations? Making politics visible. *Open Journal of Political Science, 2*(01), 1-8.

Baker, P. L. & Leicht, K. T. (2017). Globalization, Gender, and Development: Toward a Theoretical Understanding of Public Gender-Based Violence Against Women and Girls. *Sociology of Development, 3(4)*, 323-345. https://doi.org/10.1525/sod.2017.3.4.323

Barbieri, P., Bozzon, R., Scherer, S. Grotti, R., & Lugo, M. (2015). The Rise of a Latin Model? Family and fertility consequences of employment instability in Italy and Spain. *European Societies, 17(4)*, 423-446. https://doi.org/10.1080/14616696.2015.1064147

Bergman, M. M. (2007). Multimethod research and mixed methods research: old wine in new bottles? *Journal of mixed methods research, 1*(1), 101-104. https://doi.org/10.1177/1558689806291429

Bhattacherjee, A. (2012). *Social Science Research: Principles, Methods, and Practices.* Open University Press: USF Tampa Bay.

Bichi, R. (2000). *La società raccontata [The narrated society].* Milano: Franco Angeli.

Bichi, R. (2007). *L'intervista biografica. Una proposta methodologica* [The biographical interview. A methodological proposal]. Milano: Vita e pensiero.

Blee, K. M. & Taylor, V. (2002). Semi-structured interviewing in social movement research. In B. Klandermans & S. Stanggeborg (eds.) *Methods of social movement research*, (Minneapolis: University of Minnesota Press), pp. 92-117.

Bodelón, E. (2013). *Violencia de género y las respuestas de los sistemas penales* [Gender violence and the responses of the criminal justice system]. Buenos Aires, Ediciones Didot.

Bourassa, C., & Bertrand, K. (2018). Exploring the Intersection Between Violence Against Women and Children from the Perspective of Parents Convicted of

Child Homicide. *Journal of Interpersonal Violence*, 33(5), 1–22. https://doi.org/10.1177/0886260518762059

Bourdieu, P. (2001). *Masculine domination*. Cambridge, UK: Polity Press.

Brewer, J. & Hunter, A. (1989). *Multimethod research: A synthesis of styles*. Newbury Park, CA: Sage Publications, Inc.

Brewer, J.D. & Hunter, A. (2006). *Foundations of Multimethod Research: Synthesizing styles*. Thousand Oaks, CA: Sage.

Bunch, C. & Carrillo, R. (1991). *Gender Violence: A Development and Human Rights Issue*. New Brunswick: Center for Women's Global Leaders, Rutgers University.

Burt, M. R. (1980). Cultural myths and supports for rape. *Journal of Personality and Social Psychology*, 38(2), 217–230. https://doi.org/10.1037/0022-3514.38.2.217

Bustelo, M. (2016). Three decades of state feminism and gender equality policies in multi-governed Spain. *Sex Roles*, 74 (3–4), 107–120. https://doi.org/10.1007/s11199-014-0381-9

Cameron Hay, M. (2016). *Methods That Matter: Integrating Mixed Methods for More Effective Social Science Research*. University of Chicago Press.

Casique Casique, L. & Furegato, A. R. F. (2006). Violence against women: theoretical reflections. *Revista Latino-Americana de Enfermagem*, 14(16), 950-956. https://doi.org/10.1590/S0104-11692006000600018

Cavarero, A. & Rastaino, F. (2002). *Le filosofie femministe*. Torino: Paravia scriptorium.

Ciccone, S. (2017). Violenza maschile [Male violence]. *Post-filosofie, 8*, 70-81.

Cimagalli, F. (2014). *Le politiche contro la violenza di genere nel welfare che cambia. Concetti, modelli e servizi* [Policies against gender-based violence in changing welfare. Concepts, models, and services]. Milano: FrancoAngeli.

Coffey, A. (2014). Analysing Documents. In U. Flick (Ed.), *The Sage Handbook of Qualitative Data Analysis*. (pp. 367-380). London: Sage.

Collier, D. (2011). Understanding Process Tracing. *Political Science and Politics*, 44(4), 823-30. https://doi.org/10.1017/S1049096511001429

Collier, D. & Elman, C. (2008). Qualitative and Multi-Method Research: Organizations, Publication, and Reflections on Integration, in Box-Steffensmeier, J., Brady, H., Collier, D. (eds.), *Oxford Handbook of Political Methodology*. Oxford: Oxford University Press, 780-795.

Conway, J. (2016). Gender and Violence: Feminist Theories, Deadly Economies and Damaging Discourse. *E-International Relations*. https://www.e-ir.info/2017/11/03/gender-and-violence-feminist-theories-deadly-economies-and-damaging-discourse/

Corbetta, P. (1999). *Metodologia e tecniche della ricerca sociale*. Bologna: Il Mulino.

Corradi, C. & Bandelli, D. (2018). Movimenti delle donne e politiche contro la violenza. Fattori politici e sociali e specificità del caso italiano [Women's movements and policies against violence. Political and social factors and specificity of the Italian case]. In Corradi C., Fernández M.L. (2018). *Le donne nella società italiana: movimenti, politiche, medialità [Women in Italian society: movements, policies, mediality]*. Sociologia e Politiche Sociali, 21(1), FrancoAngeli.

Corradi, C. & Donato, S. (2019). Prevención y lucha contra la violencia de género en México e Italia: semántica de las leyes y desarrollo de las políticas en un análisis comparado [Prevention and fight against gender violence in Mexico and Italy: semantics of laws and policy development in a comparative analysis]. *Cultura Latinoamericana, 29 (1),* 110-136. http://dx.doi.org/10.147 18/CulturaLatinoam.2019.29.1.5

Corradi, C., & Donato, S. (2023). Movements' Dynamics and Government Responsiveness to Violence Against Women: A Study Set Against Political and Social Change in Spain and Italy. *Violence Against Women,* 107780122311 77999.

Corradi, C. & Stöckl, H. (2016). The Lessons of History. The role of the nation states and the EU in fighting violence against women in 10 European countries. *Current Sociology, 64*(4), 671-688. https://doi.org/10.1177/0011392116640457

Della Porta, D. (2003). The women's movement, the left and the State. Continuities and changes in the Italian case. In L. A. Banaszak, K. Beckwith, and D. Rucht (eds), *Women's Movements Facing the Reconfigured State,* Cambridge, Cambridge University Press, pp. 48-68.

Dogan, M. (2002), 'Strategies in Comparative Sociology', *Comparative Sociology, 1*(1), 63-92. https://doi.org/10.1163/156913202317346755

Donato, S. (2019). The Evolution of the International Documents in Fighting Violence Against Women. In Picarella, L., Truda G. (2020). *Social Systems, Cultures and Development: Fundamental Rights, Gender, Inequalities 8,* Gutenberg Edizioni– Baronissi

Donato, S. (2020). Gender-Based Violence Against Women in Intimate and Couple Relationships. The Case of Spain and Italy during the COVID-19 Pandemic Lockdown. *Italian Sociological Review, 10* (3S), 869-887. http://dx. doi.org/10.13136/isr.v10i3s.402

Easteal, P., Bartels, L., & Bradford, S. (2012). Language, gender and "reality": Violence against women, *International Journal of Law, Crime and Justice, 40* (4), 324-337. https://doi.org/10.1016/j.ijlcj.2012.05.001

EIGE, European Institute for Gender Equality. Available at: https://eige.europa.eu

EIGE, European Institute for Gender Equality (2021). Gender Equality Index. Available at: https://eige.europa.eu/gender-equality-index/2021/compare-countries (accessed 23 September 2022).

Eslen-Ziya, H. (2007). The European Union's influence on women's activist groups' networking: a comparison between Turkey and Greece. *Turkish Policy Quarterly, 6*(5), 81-88.

Esping-Andersen, G. (1990). *The three worlds of welfare capitalism.* Cambridge, UK: Polity Press.

Feci, S. & Schettini, L. (2017). *La violenza contro le donne nella storia. Contesti, linguaggi, politiche del diritto (secoli XV-XXI)* [Violence against women in history. Contexts, languages, policies of law (XV-XXI centuries)]. Roma: Viella.

Federici, S. (2018). *Caccia alle streghe, Guerra alle donne* [Witches, Witch-Hunting and Women]. Roma: Nero.

Ferrera, M. (1996). The "Southern Model" of Welfare in Social Europe. *Journal of European Social Policy, 6(1),* 17–37. https://doi.org/10.1177/095892879600 600102

Ferrera, M. (Ed.). (2005). *Welfare state reform in southern Europe: fighting poverty and social exclusion in Greece, Italy, Spain, and Portugal* (Vol. 6). New York: Routledge.

Flood, M. (2011). Involving men in efforts to end violence against women. *Men and masculinities, 14*(3), 358-377. https://doi.org/10.1177/1097184X10363995

Fraser, N. (1990). Rethinking the Public Sphere: A Contribution to the Critique of Actually Existing Democracy. *Social Text, 25/26,* 56–80.

Fraser, N. (1997). *Justice interruptus: Critical Reflections on the "postsocialist" Condition.* London: Routledge.

Fraser, N. (2009). Feminism, capitalism, and the cunning of history. *New Left Review,* 56, 97-117.

Friese, S. (2019). *Qualitative data analysis with ATLAS. ti.* London: Sage.

García, E. (2016). La génesis de la política del gobierno central contra la violencia de género [The genesis of the central government's policy against gender violence]. In La Barbera M and Cruells M (eds) *Igualdad de género y no discriminación en España: evolución, problemas y perspectivas.* Madrid: CEPC, pp.395–423.

Global Database on Violence against Women (Italy). Available at: http://evaw-global-database.unwomen.org/en/countries/europe/italy.

Global Database on Violence against Women (Spain). Available at: http://evaw-global-database.unwomen.org/en/countries/europe/spain.

González Álvarez, M. (2012). *Violencia intrafamiliar: características descriptivas, factores de riesgo y propuesta de un plan de intervención* [Domestic violence: descriptive characteristics, risk factors and proposal of an intervention plan]. Research Thesis, Universidad Complutense de Madrid, ESP.

Goodman, H. (2001). In-depth interviews. In *The handbook of social work research methods* (pp. 308-319). London: Sage.

Instituto Nacional de Estadística (INE) (2015). *Estadística de Violencia de Género* [Statistics on Gender Violence]. Available at: http://goo.gl/oWIlV6.

Istituto Nazionale di Statistica (ISTAT). *La violenza sulle donne* [Violence against women]. Available at: https://www.istat.it/it/violenza-sulle-donne.

Heise, L. (1998). Violence against women: An integrated, ecological framework. *Violence Against Women,* 4, 262-290. https://doi.org/10.1177/1077801298004003002

Hesse-Biber, S. N., & Johnson, R. B. (Eds.). (2015). *The Oxford handbook of multimethod and mixed methods research inquiry.* Oxford University Press.

Heyes, C. J. (2013). *Feminist Solidarity Across Difference: Lessons from the Women's Movement.* Oxford University Press.

Hooks, b. (1999). *Yearning: Race, Gender, and Cultural Politics.* Boston: South End Press.

Horton, J., Macve, R. & Struyven, G. (2004). Qualitative research: experience in using semi-structured interviews. In: Humphrey, Christopher and Lee, Bill H. K., (eds.) *The Real-Life Guide to Accounting Research: A Behind-The-Scenes View of Using Qualitative Research Methods.* Elsevier Science, Amsterdam, The Netherlands, pp. 339-358.

Htun, M. & Weldon, L. (2012). The Civic Origins of Progressive Policy Change: Combating Violence against Women in Global Perspective 1975-2005. *American*

Political Science Review 106(3), 548-569. https://doi.org/10.1017/S000305541 2000226

Hunter, A. D. & Brewer, J. (2015). Designing multimethod research. In S. N. Hesse-Biber, & R. B. Johnson (Eds.), *The Oxford Handbook of Multimethod and Mixed Methods Research Inquiry (Oxford Library of Psychology)* (1st edition ed., pp. 185-205). Oxford University Press.

Jewkes, R., Flood, M., & Lang, J. (2015). From work with men and boys to changes of social norms and reduction of inequities in gender relations: A conceptual shift in prevention of violence against women and girls. *The Lancet, 382*(9881), 255-266.

Kantola, J. (2006). *Feminists Theorize the State*. New York: Palgrave McMillan.

Kantola, J. (2010). *Gender and the European Union*. London: Palgrave-McMillan.

Kelly, L., Lombard, N., & Ward, I. (2005). Silence in the field: Challenges and dilemmas of qualitative research addressing gender, violence and abuse. *Qualitative Sociology Review, 1*(2), 6-26.

King, N. & Horrocks, C., & Brooks, J. (2018). *Interviews in qualitative research*. London: Sage.

Kinyanda, E., Weiss, H. A., Mungherera, M., Onyango-Mangen, P., Ngabirano, E., Kajungu, R., ... Patel, V. (2017). Gender-Based Violence and Armed Conflict: A Community-Informed Socioecological Conceptual Model From Northeastern Uganda. *Psychology of Violence*, 7(2), 267–277. https://doi.org/ 10.1037/vio0000074

Kuckartz, U. (2014). *Qualitative text analysis: A guide to methods, practice and using software*. Los Angeles: SAGE.

Kuckartz, U. (2019) Qualitative Text Analysis: A Systematic Approach. In: Kaiser G., Presmeg N. (eds) *Compendium for Early Career Researchers in Mathematics Education*. ICME-13 Monographs. Springer, Cham. https://doi.org/10.1007/ 978-3-030-15636-7_8

Kvale, S. (2007). *Doing interviews*. London: Sage.

Lacity, M. C. & Janson, M. A. (1994). Understanding Qualitative Data: A Framework of Text Analysis Methods. *Journal of Management Information Systems, 11*(2), 137-155. https://doi.org/10.1080/07421222.1994.11518043

Lagostena Bassi, T. Cappiello, A. A., & Rech, G. (1997). *Violenza sessuale 20 anni per una legge* [Sexual violence 20 years for a law]. Presidenza del Consiglio dei ministri, Commissione nazionale per la parità e le pari opportunità tra uomo e donna.

Leavy, P. (Ed.). (2014). *The Oxford handbook of qualitative research*. New York: USA, Oxford University Press.

Lombardo, E. & León, M. (2014). Políticas de igualdad de género y sociales En España: origen, desarrollo y desmantelamiento en un contexto de crisis económica [Gender equality and social policies in Spain: origin, development and dismantling in the context of economic crisis]. *Investigaciones feministas*, 5. http://dx.doi.org/10.5209/rev_INFE.2014.v5.47986

Lombardo, E., & Forest, M. (2015). The Europeanization of gender equality policies: A discursive– sociological approach. *Comparative European Politics, 13*(2), 222–239. https://doi. org/10.1057/9780230355378_1

Lombardo, E. & Rolandsen Agustín, L. (2016). Intersectionality in European Union policymaking: the case of gender-based violence. *Politics, 36(4)*, 364–373. https://doi.org/10.1177/0263395716635184

Losito, G. (2007). *L'analisi del contenuto nella ricerca sociale* [Content analysis in social research]. Milano: Franco Angeli

McBride, D. E., Mazur, A. G., Lovenduski, J., Outshoorn, J., Sauer, B., & Guadagnini, M. (2010). *The Politics of State Feminism: Innovation in Comparative Research.* Temple University Press.

Maron Young, I. (2000). *Inclusion and Democracy.* Oxford University Press.

Mazur, A. G. (2016). Toward the Systematic Study of Feminist Policy in Practice: An Essential First Step. *Journal of Women, Politics & Policy, 38(1)*, 64–83. https://doi.org/10.1080/1554477X.2016.1198210

Merry, S. E. (2009). *Gender violence: a cultural perspective.* Chichester: Wiley-Blackwell.

Ministerio del Interior, VioGén. Available at: http://www.interior.gob.es/web/servicios-al-ciudadano/violencia-contra-la-mujer/estadisticas.

Montoya, C. (2013). *From Global to Grassroots: The European Union, Transnational Advocacy, and Combating Violence against Women.* New York: Oxford University Press.

Montoya, C. (2009). International Initiative and Domestic Reforms: European Union Efforts to Combat Violence against Women. *Politics & Gender, 5(3)*, 325-348. https://doi.org/10.1017/S1743923X0999016X

Morse, J. M. (1997). *Completing a Qualitative Project: Details and Dialogue.* Thousand Oaks: Sage.

Morse, J. M. (2003). Principles of mixed methods and multi-method research design. In C. Teddlie, & A. Tashakkori (Eds.), *Handbook of mixed methods in social and behavioral research* (pp. 189-208). Thousand Oaks, CA: Sage Publication.

Nayak, M. & Suchland, S. (2006). Gender Violence and Hegemonic Projects. *International Feminist Journal of Politics, 8(4)*, 467-485. https://doi.org/10.10 80/14616740600945024

Ngozi Adichie, C. (2014). *We Should All Be Feminists.* New York: Harper Collins Publishers.

Nind M., Coverdale, A., & Meckin, R. (2021). Changing Social Research Practices in the Context of Covid-19: Rapid Evidence Review. *Project Report.* NCRM.

Parmegiani, S. & Prevedello, M. (2019*). Femminismo e femminismi nella letteratura italiana dall'Ottocento al XXI secolo* [Feminism and feminisms in Italian literature from the nineteenth to the twenty-first century]. Firenze: Società Editrice Fiorentina.

Pateman, C. (1988). *The Sexual Contract.* Stanford University Press.

Pavolini, E., León, M, Guillén, A. M., & Ascoli, U. (2015). From austerity to permanent strain? The EU and welfare state reform in Italy and Spain. *Comparative European Politics, 13(1)*, 56-76. https://doi.org/10.1057/cep.2014.41

Pettit, B., & Lee, M. (2018). Domestic violence victimization and women's health: The mediating role of depression and post-traumatic stress disorder symptoms. *Journal of Interpersonal Violence, 33(9)*, 1465-1487.

Renzetti, C. M. (2018). Feminist criminology. In J. Mitchell Miller (Ed.), *The Oxford handbook of criminological theory* (pp. 325-343). Oxford University Press.

Roggeband, C. (2012). Shifting Policy Responses to Domestic Violence in the Netherlands and Spain (1980-2009). *Violence Against Women, 18*(7), 784–806. https://doi.org/10.1177/1077801212455359

Rossi-Doria A (2005). Ipotesi per una storia che verrà [Hypothesis for a history to come]. In: Bertilotti T. & Scattigno A. (eds) *Il femminismo degli anni Settanta.* Roma: Viella, pp. 1-23.

Roth, S. (Ed.). (2008). *Gender Politics in the Expanding European Union: Mobilization, Inclusion, Exclusion.* Berghahn Books.

Ruiz-Pérez, I., & Pastor-Moreno, G. (2020). Medidas de contención de la violencia de género durante la pandemia de COVID-19 [Gender-based violence containment measures during the COVID-19 pandemic]. *Gaceta sanitaria*, S0213-9111. https://dx.doi.org/10.1016/j.gaceta.2020.04.005

Saldana, J. (2015). *The coding manual for qualitative researchers* (3rd ed.). Thousand Oaks: SAGE.

Schapp W. (2017). *Reti di Storie. L'essere dell'uomo e della cosa* [Networks of Stories. The being of the man and the thing] (a cura di D. Nuccilli). Milano: Mimesis.

Seawright, J. (2016), *Multi-Method Social Science: Combining Qualitative and Quantitative Tools (Strategies for Social Inquiry)*, Cambridge, Cambridge University Press.

Smit, B. (2002). Atlas. ti for qualitative data analysis. *Perspectives in education, 20*(3), 65-75.

Smith, J. K. (1983). Quantitative versus qualitative research: An attempt to clarify the issue. *Educational Researcher, 12(3),* 6-13. https://doi.org/10.3102/0013189X012003006

Swanton, B. (2019). The emergence of gender violence as a policy problem, in L. Sheperd (eds.), *Handbook on Gender and Violence*, Cheltenham, Edward Elgar, 160-172.

Taylor R. & Jasinski, J. L. (2011). Femicide and the Feminist Perspective. *Homicide Studies, 15*(4), 341-362. https://doi.org/10.1177/1088767911424541

Threlfall M., Cousins C., & Valiente C. (2005). *Gendering Spanish democracy.* New York: Routledge.

UNDP, United Nations Development Program (2019). *Dashboard Board 3 Women's Empowerment.* Available at: http://hdr.undp.org/en/content/dashboard-3-women's-empowerment-0 (accessed 23 September 2022).

Valiente, C. (2002). An Overview of Research on Gender in Spanish Society. *Gender & Society, 16(6),* 767–792. https://doi.org/10.1177/089124302237887

Valiente C. (2005). Combating violence against women. In: Threlfall M., Cousins C. & Valiente C. (eds). *Gendering Spanish Democracy.* New York: Routledge, pp. 101-24.

Valiente, C. (2008). Spain at the vanguard in European gender equality policies. In S. Roth (Ed.), *Gender politics in the expanding European Union: Mobilization, inclusion, exclusion* (pp. 101–117). Berghahn.

Van Esch, P. & Van Esch, L. (2013). Justification of a qualitative methodology to investigate the emerging concept: The dimensions of religion as underpinning constructs for mass media social marketing campaigns. *Journal of Business Theory and Practice, 1*(2), 214-243.

Verloo, M. M. (2005). Displacement and empowerment: Reflections on the concept and practice of the Council of Europe approach to women's rights. *Social Politics, 12*(3), 321-341.

Walby, S. (1990). *Theorizing Patriarchy*. Oxford: Basil Blackwell.

Walby, S. (2004). The European Union and Gender Equality: Emergent Varieties of Gender Regime. *Social Politics: International Studies in Gender, State & Society, 11*(1), 4-29. https://doi.org/10.1093/sp/jxh024

Walby, S., Towers, J., Balderston, S., Corradi, C., Francis, B., Heiskanen, M. & Strid, S. (2017). *The concept and measurement of violence*. Bristol: Bristol University Press.

Weldon, S. L. (2002). *Protest, Policy, and the Problem of Violence Against Women*. Pittsburgh: The University of Pittsburgh Press.

Weldon, S. L. (2006). Women's Movements, Identity Politics and Policy Impact: A study of policies on violence against women in the 50 United States. *Political Research Quarterly, 59*(1), 111-122. https://doi.org/10.1177/1065912 90605900110

Weldon, S. L. & Htun, M. (2013). Feminist Mobilisation and Progressive Policy Change: Why Governments Take Action to Combat Violence Against Women. *Gender & Development 21*(2), 231–47. https://doi.org/10.1080/13552074.2013. 802158

Wolff, S. (2004). Analysis of document and records. In Flick, U., von Kardoff, E., & Steinke, I. (Eds.), *A companion to qualitative research* (pp. 284–289). London: SAG.

Woodyatt, C. R., Finneran, C. A., & Stephenson, R. (2016). In-Person Versus Online Focus Group Discussions: A Comparative Analysis of Data Quality. *Qualitative health research, 26*(6), 741–749. https://doi.org/10.1177/1049732 316631510

World Health Organization. (2013). *Global and regional estimates of violence against women: Prevalence and health effects of intimate partner violence and non-partner sexual violence*. World Health Organization.

York, M. (2011). *Gender Attitudes and Violence against Women*. El Paso, LFB Scholarly Pub LLC.

Index